How I Escaped
The Trauma Cult
… and you can too – if you want to.

Silvia Hartmann
1st Edition 2024

**DragonRising Publishing
United Kingdom**

How I Escaped The Trauma Cult
… and you can too – if you want to.

© Text & Images Silvia Hartmann
All Rights Reserved in all media, including future media.

ISBN: 978-1-873483-91-6

Published by DragonRising Publishing UK
www.DragonRising.com

Other titles by this author:

The Energy rEvolution
EMO Energy In Motion
Modern Energy Tapping
Infinite Creativity
The Power Of The Positives
Star Matrix
StarLine Therapy

Table of Contents

1: The Cult Of Trauma 5
What Is A Cult? 6
A Matrix Built On LOVE 10

2: Love Is Real 15
The Exchange Of The Invisible Something 17
Forbidden Love – Repercussions & Cancellation 19
Psychology Fails The Love Test 21

3: Let's Dive Into The Trauma! 25
The Great Fairy Tale Of Childhood Trauma 27
The First Crack In The Great Wall Of Trauma 29

4: The Case Against Trauma 33
Where Is The Trauma? 38
False Memory Syndrome & The Infinite Trauma Generator 41

5: The Trauma Lens 47
The Danger Of Negative Journaling 49
Complex PTSD 53
The Medicalisation Of Mental Health 55

6: It's Perfectly Normal To Be An Emotional Wreck 59
The Critical Theories Or How To Ruin Anything Made Easy 61
Trauma ONLY Teaches Us What Not To Do 64
Lived Experience Doesn't Need To Be A Dirty Word 66
The Trauma Victims Race To The Bottom – And The Psychopaths Race To The Top 68
The Evil Scissors & The Trauma Cult 69

7: Microaggression, Triggers & Chronic Trauma Pain 73
Mobile Phones Murder Meaningful Connections 75
Political Correctness 80
A Few Statistics 81

8: Escaping The Fish Tank Of Insanity 83
Psychology Stole The Hope Of Healing 86
Why The Trauma Cult Destroys The Most Important

Relationships..88
Bring Back The Positive Emotions!..92
Lived experience..94

9: A Matrix Built Of Stars..95
10,000 Hours In Therapy...98
How Do You Stop All The Negativity?..................................101
We Are Not Doing Psychology, We Are Doing Modern Energy
....103
Breaking The Trauma Curse: The Timeline Of Events........105
8 Billion Prophets...109

10: Star Matrix Is The Way.....................................113
The Ultimate Heresy In The Trauma Cult............................115
A Different Kind Of Talking Therapy....................................121
Real Life Healing Made Possible At Last............................126

11: The Star Of Hope...131
The Catastrophe In Slow Motion..134
Psychology Is A Failed Field..137
The Good Therapists In The Bad Trauma Cult....................141
Walking In The Miracle Zone...145

12: I Can See Your Stars.......................................149
We Have The Power To Create Stars..................................152
The True Meaning Of Ascension..155
From A New Past There Arises A New Future....................160
Love & Logic..162
Start Today – Star Matrix Is The Way!.................................164

1: The Cult Of Trauma

In 2011, I had my moment of perfect clarity when I realised that I had been trapped in an extremely destructive and unhealthy cult – the cult of trauma.

Some call this cult "psychology" and I thought it was that too at first; but psychology is simply a reflection of a greater malady that goes deep down into philosophy and how human beings have constructed their cults across the ages.

Psychology is, however, the shop front for the cult of trauma, and certainly bears much responsibility for the continuing recruitment, and the development of ever more radical wings of the cult, which are ever more destructive in turn.

In this book, I am going to lay out for you, my dear and highly intelligent reader, how I came to understand that I had been, indeed, trapped in a cult. You can compare this to your own life's experiences, your true lived experience as opposed to what we are taught is right and true; and I will also lay out the simple route to escape this dreadful cult that does nothing beneficial for the human spirit.

Having listened to a number of people who escaped from various cults, particularly from Scientology, and noting that they went essentially from one cult to the other, we need to start with the idea of what a cult is, what it does, and why people join a cult.

What Is A Cult?

"Cult" is the derogatory term for a thought matrix that has fewer followers than the mainstream cult which is operating the entire society within which they exist.

The thought matrix is a system of beliefs about the nature of the universe, the world, and what human beings are.

Without such a thought matrix, human beings cannot function.

This is extremely important to understand – we NEED a thought matrix or we will go completely insane.

In order not to have to write "thought matrix" over and over, I am now going to refer to this simply as "The Matrix."

Please be advised that no matter how free thinking and free willed you believe yourself to be, it is impossible to operate as a human being without a Matrix.

Essential questions such as, "Who am I? Where do I come from? Where am I going? What is the purpose of life? Why am I here? What is right, and what is wrong? How do I know what to do under these circumstances?" need to be answered, one way, or the other.

Any Matrix is composed of such fundamental high level components, and all the rules within that Matrix flow from these high level components.

For example, the United States of America has a "constitution" which does not include specific laws, but is a high level framework, a Matrix, which creates all the sub-laws within it.

I am the originator of Modern Energy, and at some point, I became aware that I was building a Matrix. This terrified me, as the very last thing I ever wanted to be is a "cult leader" and the very last thing I ever wanted for the people who applied my work was to become "cult followers."

I thought about this for many decades and finally came to the following conclusions.

1. The current Matrices are not healthy. They are extremely destructive and they do NOT serve "the people," neither on the personal, individual level, not on the societal level, nor on the inter-societal levels. If you doubt me, take a look both at the history of the human race as well as turn on the news, right here, right now.
2. I am building a new Matrix.
3. I am trying to build a BETTER Matrix than the ones which are currently operating.
4. As a human being, it is my absolute right to attempt to build a new Matrix, as all Matrices ever were created by other human beings, too.

That was a big relief.

It took me to the next question, which was, "How do you build a Matrix that is more beneficial to humanity? How could you ever know that you're not building in something that seems like a good idea at the time?"

"How can you tell right from wrong?"

Here, to my rescue, came the Modern Energy Chart.

The Modern Energy Chart[1] is a representation of how people change depending on their "happiness."

In brief, the "happier" people are, the more empowered they become; the more intelligent, the more reasonable and the more rational.

At +10, LOVE and LOGIC become one and the same, and we are in the best position to know the most.

So I made the core of my Matrix about making people happier, the shorthand term for improving their emotional states of being.

---

1 For more information about the Modern Energy Chart and Modern Energy, please see "The Energy rEvolution" by Silvia Hartmann, free to download from GoE.ac/revolution and available to purchase as hardcopy from all good bookstores, online and off.

If something moves a person up on the Modern Energy Chart, that is a good thing, and we are going in the right direction.

If something moves a person down the Modern Energy Chart, into the states of stress, anxiety, anger and depression, that is a bad thing.

With this simple guiding mechanism in place, we can now assess the effects of techniques, methods, laws, ideas - and matrices.

A Matrix Built On LOVE

A good question to ask of any matrix is, "Where is the love?"

Is there talk about love?

Is this love expressed in the laws of the matrix?

Does it work in practice?

Are the members of that matrix loving among each other, and with other matrices that exist?

Is this practice of love born out in practical, beneficial results in success, health, happiness in Mind, Body & Spirit of the inhabitants of that matrix?

How far is the theory and practice of that matrix diverging from actual reality?

What I mean by that is there are many matrices which preach one thing, but behind closed doors, DO something completely different.

That is a reality divergence, and a sign that there's something not quite right with that matrix, because all the actions of the inhabitants flow directly from the laws of the matrix.

The psychology matrix is quite unique, possibly in the entirety of human history, in that it is the only one that functions completely without love of any kind.

Please take a moment, take a deep breath, and let's repeat that statement.

The psychology matrix is quite unique, possibly in the entirety of human history, in that it is the only one that functions completely without love of any kind.

How it came to be that something that calls itself "The Study of the Soul" or even, "The Science of the Soul" has been trying to get by without a word about "love" for over a century is incomprehensible, and I personally do not dwell on this.

With psychology, we have a matrix, a cult, that doesn't have any love in it whatsoever.

The concept itself is absent; there is no definition of emotions; there is neither a desire to understand emotions, to research them, or even work with them in any meaningful way.

There is, however, a single rule, the one ring that rules them all, namely that "Trauma is the cause of all human suffering and the singular cause for all human negative emotions."

This absolutely myopic focus on trauma as the new "Satan of modern humanity" is beyond limiting, beyond destructive, beyond illogical – it creates a spiral of insanity that gets worse and worse until people break as they try to operate within that matrix.

Please be advised that NOW, I can see that clearly.

You have to be outside any matrix to see the problems with it; whilst you are inside of it, inside the cult, all the insanity appears perfectly normal.

At this point, I would like us to note that all cult "survivors" know this, and have experienced this for themselves.

You enter into any Matrix, and everything that happens there, no matter how insane, it seems perfectly reasonable. It may even for a long time make a person feel better than they did before.

A recently "escaped" Scientologist was super happy and reported that his old life never made sense but now he realises that he has ADHD, detachment disorder, and Complex PTSD and he's never been happier.

The audience clapped and cheered; I thought, "Wow. He's gone straight from one cult to the other ..."

There are many, many more such matrices than we are currently aware of.

If you look across your life, you will find that you have joined many "cults" as well already, and left them at some point. Perhaps you were an enthusiastic member of a "gamer's community," or you went to India for a major Yoga retreat. Perhaps you joined a club for knitters, or flower arrangers, or rabbit breeders, or a political party – there's always a matrix at play, what you can and cannot do, how it all works, and we spend time there, fully immersed, and then drift away again.

It's not like we are either in a cult, or out of it. We are always, always engaging in various matrices, big and small – every human being does that, and especially nowadays, as there are so many different types on offer.

The most insidious types of matrix, however, are those "fish tanks of insanity" in which we swim, they're everywhere, all around us, expressed in all the modalities of human endeavour, and we are completely unaware that we are inside a destructive cult, inside a matrix.

I had no idea that I too was inside the grand Psychology Trauma Matrix until the moment when I woke up to it.

This is my story.

2: Love Is Real

In 1993, I was working as an assistant researcher for an animal behaviour consultant's association in the UK. We were given the task to conduct a research study on aggressive dog behaviour, and whether changing the aggressive dog's diet would improve their behaviour.

I was young, enthusiastic, loved the scientific method and eager; as an animal behaviour specialist at the end of a referral chain, I had access to a big group of aggressive dogs and their owners and set to work.

Little did my naïve aspect know that the study was paid for by an international pet food conglomerate who wanted to add the promise of "improving your dog's behaviour, proven by this scientific study here ..." to their global marketing campaigns.

The study worked as follows. The aggressive dog's diet was changed to that company's dried kibble, and results were taken from the owners over a period of two weeks.

And the results were amazing. Over 80% of the owners reported a measurable improvement in their dog's behaviour in general.

However, my young aspect did not stop when the study was completed and the data was handed over.

She had many questions about this whole thing, and so she started to conduct her own studies.

This involved changing the diet for the next group of aggressive dogs to other things, from natural food such as raw meat to the cheapest, nastiest kinds of canned mush; and it also involved staying in contact with the owners of the original research dogs past the two week cut off limit.

From this, I found out two things.

No. 1 was that the benefits from the original dog food flattened out after two weeks, and by four weeks, the dogs had returned fully to their previous behaviours.

No. 2 was that it didn't make any difference at all what you changed the dog's diet to – just so long as the owners changed it, there was a noticeable improvement in the behaviour across the board. These changes also flattened out predictably after two or more weeks.

It was here that the young Silvia began to wonder whether there was an additional component at play here, and that it wasn't the change in food that made the difference, but in fact, something that happened with the owners when they changed the dog's food.

The idea arose that the change in the dogs was happening because the owners were asked questions about their dog's behaviours, and as a result, paid more attention to their dogs than before.

This idea – the effect of ATTENTION on the behaviour of pet animals – started a research ball rolling that eventually led us to where we are today.

The Exchange Of The Invisible Something

Attention – a person looking directly at a companion animal, as the first step towards an interaction with them, had strange and miraculous seeming side effects.

It was like something invisible was given, which the animal craved, and needed for their health and happiness.

"Attention seeking behaviour" could be clearly seen to escalate, and eventually end in violence, when the attempts to get "attention" were ignored.

This was a real "thing."

It was invisible, but there was something those animals really needed, and which could literally drive them crazy if they didn't get it – there was an invisible something being exchanged here that was as important to health and happiness as was food and water.

Once you understood that animals were craving the invisible something, and when they were given attention, their behaviours would change, reliably and in the same pattern, even across species of companion animals, you could see the effects of the invisible something everywhere.

Of course, it wasn't long before my researchers and I started to notice that the exact same patterns of exchanges also played out between us and our partners, our children, and other people in general.

The invisible something had a lot to answer for.

We discussed it, we played with it.

We found that if you give more attention, not just to stop unwanted behaviours, but simply additional "rations" of positive attention, the animals really started to transform, and relationships blossomed. It was amazing, and we were super excited about this.

More and more evidence and experience piled up, until the day came and I finally put two and two together – the invisible something was LOVE.

Love is real.

The presence of love alleviates behaviour problems.

The absence of love directly causes behaviour problems.

My young aspect was super excited by this discovery and entirely unaware that in that moment, she had fallen out of not only the existing animal behaviour matrix, not only out of the existing psychology matrix, but out of the entire scientific materialistic reductionist paradigm all at the same time.

Forbidden Love – Repercussions & Cancellation

One of the saddest moments of my life came when I, full of excitement at the discovery that love is actually real, and the great big missing X Factor in animal behaviour research, ran into her office and to a big book shelf which contained almost everything that had ever been written about animal behaviour studies in the English language, usually conducted in the context of trying to figure out human behaviour.

She took one book, one research paper after the other off the shelf and tried to find that word, LOVE.

As dusk fell, and it became too dark to see the pages, I woke up in a sea of books on the carpet.

A sea of books, and not one contained the word, LOVE.

The big book shelf was completely empty now.

New books would have to be written.

The next day, my aspect wrote "The Harmony Program[i]," which explains how to use the power of attention, the power of LOVE, to transform animal behaviour problems. It also outlines how the industry standard, the "Dominance Reduction Programs" were actually harmful to the relationship between animals and owners, and should be abandoned forthwith.

When she took her findings to her research leader, she expected the man to be just as excited as she had been. He looked at it, and she knew he understood, and knew that she was right.

He turned red, started to sweat and then screamed at her, "If you think I am going to rewrite all my books now, you've got another thing coming!"

He threw her out of his office, and then set about to have her cancelled from the entire field of companion animal behaviour.

Her name was blackened as a crazy person; she could no longer get published in any magazine or journal; not only was she forbidden entrance to congresses and conferences, her students were told in no uncertain terms to never, ever mention her name or her work again.

That was that.

Now, I take a measure of pride in having being cancelled decades before it became as fashionable as it is today; that I have survived that, and that I am still speaking about something that is perfectly true, perfectly observable, perfectly replicable and which would help so, so many if only they knew about it.

The field of animal behaviour being closed now, where to go next?

Psychology seemed to be the perfect answer.

Behaviour problems in companion animals are one thing; but behaviour problems in human children are so much more important to be solved.

Surely, the field of psychology would be delighted to learn that there really is such a thing as love, and if that is completely real and provable, perhaps even this mysterious "the soul" which gave the entire field its title, might be as well?

Psychology Fails The Love Test

The first step to get into any "field" is to buy some books and to read them, at least this was the way in 1993.

As you can probably imagine by now, I could not read any of the great psychology books by the various founders without particularly looking for that one single word, LOVE.

As you might or might not know through personal experience, we do not have to say much more about how psychology failed the Love Test.

There was more, however.

The ideas and concepts expressed in these books were so endlessly convoluted, so utterly peculiar and at the same time, so reality removed, it was painful.

If you take the greatest driver of human thought and behaviour out of the equation, you have to constantly calculate around the enormous elephant, nay mammoth in the room of humanity – emotions.

If you don't know how to explain emotions, of course you will be writing crazy things.

That is completely unavoidable.

"The mammoth in the room of humanity."

When you literally don't know what you're doing, and then try talking and writing about that, of course it's going to become exactly the kind of thing you find in the psychology books – and all of it, at the end of the day, is of course completely useless downstream to the people who don't understand what's going on with them, with their emotions, with their lives.

Not long ago, I saw a professor of psychology, who had become addicted to various psychopharmaceutical medications during his study to become a professor of psychology over 20 years ago.

He was now telling others about his attempts to start a withdrawal program.

This is what I mean about this particular field of study being completely useless "downstream" - if that which you are studying isn't helping you, how is it going to help anyone at all?

What is the point of it beyond making money from clients who never get any better?

I would ask myself these questions, completely unaware still just how completely brainwashed we all are, immersed in our trauma therapy culture, as we are.

In 1993, I didn't think psychology was the way forward for me and my revolutionary love inclusive approaches, so I did something else instead[ii].

In order to help people, now we have to deal with talking therapy.

And what are we going to talk about?

Naturally, of course, this is going to be all about trauma, right ..?

3: Let's Dive Into The Trauma!

In 1998, I found EFT – Emotional Freedom Techniques, the simplified version of Thought Field Therapy by Dr Roger Callahan, a clinical Psychologist, who had taken the technique from a gentleman called Jim Diamond, and used it exclusively to treat trauma, as any good psychologist would.

I was delighted. Finally, finally a way to work directly with energy.

Tapping on meridians, energy flows in the real energy body, to remove energy blockages.

Where did these blockages come from?

Well, trauma, of course!

Many existing psychologists, fed up with not having anything to actually help their clients with their trauma, took to tapping therapies and started to call themselves "Energy Psychologists."

I thought of that as a nice try, but seeing that psychology doesn't accept that there is such a thing as an energy body in the first place, I personally could not see Energy Psychology being embraced by the general psychologists, or to be allowed into the hallowed halls of "Psychology Science."

I gave that little heed because I was busy with finding out more about why people do the things they do.

EFT was fascinating[iii].

In the hands of an intuitive practitioner you could turn a spider phobia into a love for spiders in under an hour. Cure a fear of flying. A fear of elevators, of clowns, of balloons, of injection needles or of heights. Even all manner of allergic responses could be worked with, as well as psychosomatic problems and all the many negative emotions.

The fact is that a person who gets frightened by a dog as a child can become very afraid of dogs; and when we tap on these meridian points and improve the flow of energy through the living energy body, that fear recedes and never comes back in its original form.

I would like to point out that this is still the case; so if you ever meet anyone who has a specific phobia or fear of anything specific, send them to someone who does Modern Energy Tapping. It will solve that particular problem for them.

The Great Fairy Tale Of Childhood Trauma

Soon enough, instead of focusing on a single problem, people would want to change their lives with EFT.

At the time, I didn't realise this, but the entire population is programmed to think there's something wrong with them, something that happened in childhood, and if only they could remember that and talk about it for long enough, or release it with EFT tapping, their lives would change immediately and they could live happily, ever after.

This is a strange kind of fairy tale, deep at the bottom of the trauma quest, and we will return to this later.

Now we have an endless stream of clients who want to tap on their traumas to radically change their lives for the better.

EFT brought something to the psychology party that had never been known before – the ability to release any trauma in a single session.

This was completely unheard of in psychology, where one single trauma can be discussed for years, literally, and it never "releases" at all to the point where the client just laughs and says, "Ah, that's so in the past, I am so over that!"

EFT tapping however, did just that.

A single practitioner could see 40 clients in a week, and release their traumas. A single client could do ten tapping sessions in a week, and release ten traumas.

And yet, and curiously, nothing much changed in their lives at all.

Wait a minute!

What about that fairy tale? About that person whose life had sucked because when they were three years old, they fell off a swing? And by releasing this formative trauma, now their life doesn't suck any more, and they get to live happily, ever after?

This was NOT happening, and the longer the tapping experiment went on, the more this became apparent.

There were also problems that did not get solved by tapping on trauma, or by trying to find the specific trauma that might have caused the problem.

The First Crack In The Great Wall Of Trauma

Here, I tell the story of my personal moment of enlightenment on that topic, which was the lady who ate buckets of strawberry ice cream when she felt lost and lonely.

As I enquired into this, she told the story of sitting with her father on a bench by the seaside. He has bought her a strawberry ice cream. The wind is cold; she shivers.

He puts his arm around her and she feels warmed, loved and protected, happier than she had ever been before, just at the same moment as her tongue makes contact with the strawberry ice cream.

That was the moment when I discovered another form of driver for an existing problem – it was a happy event, a Guiding Star, which caused the problem in the Here & Now.

That was in 2000[iv], and once again, my aspect was hugely excited by this discovery.

The very idea of happy events being the absolute "root cause" of a behavioural problem Here & Now was, once again, heresy in the trauma cult.

As always, I thought that my research had something beneficial to offer to those who want to help other people, and in general, have a better understanding of how and why people do the things they do, but once again, nobody took any notice, and the trauma tapping went on as before.

Personally, I became fascinated by the FACT that people do not just have trauma events, but clearly, also

Guiding Star events, and began to wonder what other kinds of events happen in people's lives, and how they influence behaviour over entire lifetimes.

That was really interesting, and I spent eight years on finding out more about this. I learned a lot, wrote up my findings in the attempt to share the insights derived from this period of research, and the techniques we can use to deal with a variety of events. "Events Psychology[v]" was published in 2008, and as the Harmony Program before it, was entirely ignored.

If it isn't trauma, it doesn't even exist ...

I still did not realise how deep and wide the trauma cult really was; but that moment came in 2011, when I was teaching a correspondence course for professional energy tapping, which I called Energy EFT[vi].

There is a Unit on tapping for trauma; and the next Unit deals with treating Guiding Stars that are causing problems in the Here & Now, such as philias, fetishes and addictions.

In this Unit on Guiding Stars, in which every exercise, every method, every technique and every example was about GUIDING STAR events, as the homework exercise it was set to "Treat an event of your own."

I particularly phrased it as "treat an EVENT" so I could pick up any student who would try to treat some trauma once more, just to be on the safe side.

What happened was that the first few students, all of whom had immediately treated a trauma again, made me laugh. 20 or so students who all failed to treat a Guiding Star, and I was becoming scared.

By the time all 197 students had ALL immediately fallen back into trauma, I had begun to realise just how bad this actually was.

How widespread the trauma entrainment was, how deeply rooted.

I also realised that I was still doing the same thing.

Whenever anything went wrong, I would reflexively start wondering what trauma in my childhood that was related to.

This wasn't just me, either.

I became aware of how the trauma culture infused everything, everywhere and all the time.

Songs about trauma.

Movies with heroes and villains whose motivation is trauma.

Social media feeds with trauma based memes.

Trauma based art.

Trauma poetry.

Trauma as the only possible explanation for literally everything.

It is extraordinary once you start to see it – and that's before what was the general trauma cult swirling away in the background became the breeding ground for a radical ideology that weaponises trauma swept the globe.

The trauma cult is a cult, it is a matrix.

It is incredibly destructive to those caught within it.

However, once we understand that, there is an easy way out. We'll come to that in a little while.

Before we do, allow me to make my case against trauma in principle.

4: The Case Against Trauma

Before we start, let us come together in the truth about trauma.

Trauma is quite real, and it affects people's behaviour.

How that works is completely mysterious and inexplicable in the reality reduced Mind/Body five sense paradigm; when we bring in the living energy body, it's simple.

Something happens to upset or disturb the energy body, and now it is injured and produces symptoms in the form of negative emotions, which directly causes disturbed thinking and disturbed behaviour.

When these energy body disturbances are alleviated, the emotions change for the better, and so does the thinking, and the behaviours.

It's nice and simple as a theory, and works a treat in practice.

However, when your only tool is a hammer, every problem becomes a nail, and thus it is with psychology and trauma.

There is only trauma.

Trauma is taking all the attention, all the investigation.

Therein lies the problem.

When you tune to trauma, remember trauma, think or talk about trauma, the energy body reacts to this negatively.

The energy body becomes destabilised, stressed. This affects the entire totality, so the mind and the body become stressed as well and at the same time, adding their stress to the system.

This has innumerable side effects.

The body shuts down digestion under stress, for example.

I've discovered that the energy system shuts down its own natural functions under stress also.

Obviously, we can tell that the brain and the mind are negatively affected, because the more stressed we are, the more illogical and irrational we become in a direct cause-and-effect relationship.

This is a dangerous, severe disturbance of the totality which produces all manner of unwanted occurrences across the board; but it isn't even the end of the story.

Once the totality is out of stress, it takes a lot of time and energy to try and recover to a more harmonious state. The more often these highly destructive stress states happen, the longer it takes to recover; and in extreme cases, the totality doesn't recover at all any longer.

People know this, and that is why they don't want to access trauma memories. They will naturally do whatever they can not to go there, and not to trigger these negative, dangerous responses.

This is our first evidence against wilfully and repeatedly accessing trauma.

Accessing trauma memories is extremely destructive to the totality, not just to the energy system.

People have to be trained hard, brainwashed, into accessing trauma through the promise that their life will get better if only they do this, and of course, we are.

The idea of having to do bad, painful things before anything gets better is deeply and profoundly programmed into us, and not just via pop psychology since the 1920s.

For example, I saw a social media post the other day, with half a million "likes," that stated, "You have to descend to ascend."

You need to delve into your trauma, into your "shadow side," into the worst experiences of your life, into your own worst qualities and shortcomings, before you have any chance whatsoever to be healed, to feel better, or to be loved by the Universe.

I want you to stop for a moment and think about how preposterous that is.

In order to get to A, you have to go to B.

You can't get to A without going to B first.

Why can't we go to A? Because you can never get to A without going to B first.

You can never be happy unless you deal with all of your trauma first.

That's the underlying idea in the trauma cult, and everyone who is in the trauma cult, accepts this idea without question. It's the truth, right? It's the only truth of human existence ...

Now I couldn't say just how many people have been in talking therapy and for how long, discussing their various traumas, in the world of human beings in the last 100 years, but I am not seeing a corresponding increase in enlightened human beings.

There's a whole lot of exclusive "descending" going on, but without any sign of "ascending" at the end of it.

In other words, this isn't working, is it?

The very fact that 75 years ago people did not raise their hands to say "This isn't working!" shows us clearly that the idea of "having to descend before we can ascend" was already programmed into the matrix that was active at the time.

Psychology is simply the latest variation on the topic.

The monks in the middle ages used to wear hair shirts and flagellate themselves with whips in their attempts to descend; now we do it with words and memories, and it's still as unattractive, as unloving and as crazy as it ever was.

Now let us return to the core fact here, namely that every time a person accesses any kind of trauma memory deliberately, their energy system gets extremely stressed, their digestion shuts down instantly, and their mind will produce all manner of nonsense because they can no longer think clearly.

By going to a therapist once a week to talk about trauma, or attending a psychology based self help meeting of any kind, or even by starting a pop psychology talk with a friend, we put more stress on our already highly stressed systems.

There are many people who find it doesn't help them, and many more who don't want to do this in the first place, and again, we might want to ask why nobody is saying, "Can we do something else please? This isn't making me feel any better."

The reason there is no alternative to psychology is the trauma cult itself.

Even those who don't want to participate, or have tried and failed to find anything good about it, don't realise that there is a problem with the trauma worship itself, and will still recommend the established trauma based approaches to others, believing it was something about them which caused these processes to fail.

Where Is The Trauma?

The true belief in the reality of trauma as the be all and end all to human experience and behaviour is beautifully played out in a cult from the 1950s that focused their efforts to root out all the trauma, once and for all.

You take out all your trauma, and you will ascend into an enlightened state of being that will give you superpowers, and save the world.

Sounds good?

So let's go and find the trauma!

It is fascinating that when a person starts with this, they will get some "gains," just like those dogs did in that old commercial dog food study. In that study, I ended up attributing the "gains" to the additional attention the dogs were receiving from their owners.

A person starts with their psychology based trauma therapy, and they do get additional attention from their therapists. I am smiling as I am writing this, as what I want to say here is that they get additional energy - or using that most controversial word LOVE - from their therapists.

As with all relationships, they are the most intense when they first begin, in the first flush of romance, and the intensity of the attention being paid lessens naturally over the course of the interactions.

Let us remember that we have a person here who has some problems in their life right here, right now, and they are seeking some kind of evolution.

They are now directed to their various traumas which are the one and only reason for their problems right here, right now.

After the first flush of romance, the gains start to flatten out.

Is this taken as evidence that this isn't working?

No! Not at all! The problem is that we haven't found the right trauma yet.

Let's dig deeper!

No significant gains. No enlightenment experiences. No true Miracle Expansions.

This can go on for years and years, still nobody questions the core principle that we can find the causative trauma and then everything will get better.

In the meantime, the additional life energy, attention, from a good therapist helps to feed the client's energy body and can make them feel better; and this is taken as the proof of concept, when in fact, it is natural human interaction that is creating the benefits, and the methodology is stealing the credit and using it illegally to shore up its faulty premises.

If you do an awful lot of this trauma questing, like the aforementioned 1950s trauma based cult who do this every single day for years on end, or if you use meridian tapping, which can also flatten out trauma memories in a single session, you run out of easily accessible trauma from this life eventually.

This however, is never taken as a hint that perhaps the whole trauma thing in and of itself is nothing but a wild goose chase. That this never happens is another sign of the power of that Trauma Matrix, and just how totally immersed everyone is within it.

What happens if you run out of trauma but you haven't ascended?

Well now … perhaps the trauma is repressed trauma, meaning it is trauma that was so terrible, you can't possibly consciously remember it.

OK …

I am not saying that such a thing as repressed trauma isn't possible or doesn't exist. I would make the point however that if the (unknown, undiscovered, misunderstood, under-explored) human totality functions to naturally repress things that are too bad to handle or too disabling to remember, perhaps there's a reason for that.

Perhaps the system is saying, "No, don't do that, it's dangerous!" is something we should listen to?

Just a thought …

Digging deep for that elusive repressed trauma had its heyday in the mid 1980s, when we got "false memory syndrome."

False Memory Syndrome & The Infinite Trauma Generator

Here, therapists who were particularly keen and dedicated on "finding the trauma" started to hypnotise their clients, give them leading suggestions, and the clients' dear Energy Minds[2] responded by creating extremely creative scenarios of abuse, as they would.

Our dear Energy Minds, previously known as the unconscious or subconscious minds, and what I consider to be simply the brain and neurology of the living energy body, are the generators of infinite creativity.

You ask them a question, and they will answer.

I learned this during the negative EFT tapping times with clients who would ask themselves every single day, "What's wrong with me?" and the dear Energy Mind would answer, every day, with ever more creative scenarios of wrongness.

This led to some of the most extraordinary Opening Statements I had ever heard, for example, a German man was tapping on, "Even though I was born from a race of genocidal maniacs, I deeply and profoundly love and accept myself."

The great mistake of the people who were asking, "What's wrong with me?" every day, sometimes three times a day, was that they were not dealing with a bucket

---

2 I understand the ENERGY MIND to be simply the brain and neurology of the living energy body – to replace the negative ideas of a "sub" or "un" conscious mind. I add the "dear" to the phrase "dear Energy Mind" to give it some love, some attention, and to learn that it is simply a natural system that's designed to help us out in life. There's much merit in being polite to your own mind, body and spirit!

that you could eventually empty out, but instead with an infinity generator which will never, ever stop, and become crazier and crazier, the more you do that.

In the meantime, the "memories that are so terrible that we had to repress them or we would go insane and those are the reasons why your life is a mess" were silently taken off the table for now, but their scary shadow remained, swirling around amid the trauma cult entrained, and it's still swirling, even as we speak.

So what are we to do, now that we've run out of accessible this-life-trauma, the repressed-this-life trauma is too scary, but we haven't found the source of trauma that would explain it all … yet?

Well, there was a big fashion for prenatal trauma, pre-birth trauma and also birth itself trauma for a while, with people screaming, writhing and abreacting. This would predictably cause even more stress in the totality, negative side effects and all that; and of course, it didn't fix anything that was troubling the persons who partook in this in their real lives, here and now.

Where is the trauma?

Now here's a good idea – it's not your trauma, you've inherited it from your family, from your ancestors. Let's work with that for a few decades.

Did it fix anything at all?

No. It just made the people who partook in it even sadder, even angrier, even more disturbed. The entire enormous timeline of any person's ancestors, going back millions of years, and all that trauma focused in on the living lens that is the one lonely person struggling here and now, wow, that's a lot of trauma to be dealing with.

And yet, it still wasn't enough, and the endless chase to find THE trauma that would fix it all and bring about that total rebirth into a life filled with happiness continued.

Perhaps it wasn't the this-life trauma. Perhaps it wasn't the direct ancestral trauma heritage. Perhaps it was … drum roll please … yes, Past Life Trauma!

All this time, there were people trying to improve themselves, improve their lives. They were highly motivated to find something that could help them, a way of being, feeling and thinking, and they were willing to put their totality through all manner of pain, suffering and horror, just so something good would emerge at the end of this.

I want us to stop right here and take a moment to appreciate all these people who were engaging in this, from all sides, doing the very best they could to bring about positive evolution, healing, an emergence of a better way of being.

Don't laugh at the cult survivors. Appreciate them for their spirit and their attempts to make the world a better place, to make their worlds a better place.

All of us are children, trying to find our way in the Great Creative Order.

None of us can do any better than just to give our best efforts, and even though it often doesn't seem that way, we all do.

Let us not laugh at the millions of people who went earnestly on their quests to discover the terrible traumas in their past lives that are stopping them from being the wonderful being they want to be right here, right now.

Let us simply note that in the 1950s cult, they really went for it. A past life a day, for years and more.

Now as we have already observed, past lives are a form of content that is generated endlessly by our dear Energy Mind, just for the asking.

The more you ask, the more readily the dear Energy Mind responds; and if you keep asking for past life trauma, and your totality is getting stressed, what the Energy Mind produces becomes more and more disturbing in a direct cause-and-effect connection.

In that 1950s cult particularly, where earnest practitioners ask their very earnest clients about their past lives for the 500th time, what happened was that the dear Energy Mind was generating now stories of strange aliens, zombies, dragons and all sorts of things that were pretty unlikely to have happened in any lived past life experience on Planet Earth.

Now where's that trauma coming from?

Well … that would be … parallel past lives, or future lives, parallel or otherwise, from anywhere in the multiverse …

That's the final admission that the trauma is never ending, and that you will never get to the end and will never find that trauma that causes you to be who you are, right here, right now.

All those horror stories, first person associated, of course bring the totality down every time, so we can now expect people who have gone through this to have serious psychosomatics, immune system related illnesses, and thinking some very crazy thoughts, plus the aforementioned emotional instability and some whole new symptoms they had never experienced before.

And still, in spite of all of this, nobody ever challenged the trauma core of the cult.

Isn't that just extraordinary?

5: The Trauma Lens

Nothing explains the destructive effect of the Trauma Lens better than the following joke:

What is Irish Alzheimer's?

When you only remember the insults.

I laughed for a long time when I first heard that, and was immediately reminded of my great aunt Annie, who suffered from this particular affliction.

After attending any family gathering, she would go through what happened AFTERWARDS in her mind and look for insults.

Moments of disrespect, a wayward glance, comments that might have meant something else, something bad, something insulting, or something that should have been said but wasn't - she would come up with all sorts of things. She would wind herself up with talking about these perceived insults and then decide to hate certain family members forever – who had literally no idea why, or what had happened there.

This is the deadly long term effect of the trauma lens.

You can look at any relationship at all, no matter who or what with, and if you sort only for the insults, the "trauma," you will destroy that relationship.

That's simply a fact.

It is how the human systems work; it's natural, it is even realistic.

We gather evidence and then base our decisions upon that evidence.

With the trauma lens, we only gather the negative evidence.

"How was your relationship with your father?"

Let's say we have an average Jo father and an average Jo descendant.

For 18 years, client Jo lived in Father Jo's house and had many experiences along the way.

What happens if we spent a year, just one year, focusing only on the trauma inflicted by Jo on Jo?

What does that do to the relationship between Jo and Jo?

What we have here is an ongoing trial, where not only is there no evidence presented in defence, the very concept that there could be a defence is absent altogether. In such a scenario, and in the complete absence of any information that could challenge this singular point of view, of course the jury will have to convict, every time.

Is such a one sided trial fair? Will it produce truth, or justice?

Let's talk about negative journaling here for a moment.

The Danger Of Negative Journaling

The more active members in the trauma cult are encouraged to write down their stressed thoughts in what I call a negative journal.

Of course, they wouldn't be writing down their good experiences that day; like my great aunt Annie, they would only and exclusively focus on all the insults instead.

Imagine our friend Jo from the last chapter, creating their trauma based journal about their relationship with their father.

It would be a laundry list of terrible things that the father had done or failed to do that spans at least the 18 years Jo spent in the father's house, but most likely extending far beyond that and going on for as many years as Jo has been alive.

Now imagine Jo would not just journal about their father, but their mother, their siblings, their uncles and aunts, the next door neighbours, teachers and politicians, school mates, friends, colleagues, strangers …

What a journal that would be!

Can you get a sense of how such a thing could gather steam, become a vortex of more and more negativity that can soon enough turn into high stress, anxiety, paranoia and then flip into outright rage, hate and aggression?

Why, that would be just like the journals of the school shooters in the US, ending up with a crazy manifesto that calls for blood …

There is this unfortunate idea that if we can somehow "vomit out the trauma," the trauma will be gone and we will be clear.

This doesn't actually work.

It really does not.

I had an artist friend who always painted the same picture. A self portrait with a bloody Jesus on the cross as the eyebrows and nose, in black and red.

Over the years I knew him, these pictures became ever more stress riddled, spikey, crazy, disturbing. Everybody knew that he had been sexually abused by a Catholic priest and that's why he was painting those pictures all the time.

He had literally painted thousands of them by the time I walked into his studio that day. He was at it again, stabbing violently at the canvas with the paint brush, and on that occasion, I couldn't take it any more and shouted at him, "You've been painting the bloody problem for years now – why don't you paint the solution?"

In that moment, Modern Energy Art Solutions[3] was born, and I am happy to say that the artist in question never painted the old picture ever again.

---

3   Art & Energy together are absolutely fascinating. Check out EnergyArt.uk if you love art – and energy!

Let me be clear about this. "Vomiting out" your pain doesn't work.

It doesn't matter if you pour your pain into a song, a poem, a painting, an online rant, howling at your therapist for 55 minutes, or into negative journaling.

It does not work. It doesn't change anything, it doesn't make anything better, and over time, it will destroy your energy system and the rest of your totality.

What tends to happen is that people just get exhausted and stop because they can't do it any longer. And that's the best to hope for. With my artist friend's paintings becoming ever more violent, would it have been possible that one day he would have taken a knife to a random priest instead of stabbing at the canvas with the brush in his clenched fist?

51

Negative journaling can be extremely dangerous not just to an individual's long term health and happiness, but to society at large. It also reinforces the trauma cult's obsessions as trauma art is being displayed in public spaces, museums and celebrated by selling for ridiculous sums of money.

This, once again, is never acknowledged or addressed within the all encompassing trauma cult. We need to keep talking about trauma, thinking about trauma, finding more trauma, more and more and more trauma …

But where does that lead us?

Complex PTSD

Right now, we have a new trauma diagnosis.

A real trauma diagnosis is PTSD, such as experienced by people who have been in extreme situations and came away with severe injuries to their energy systems.

Of course, according to the trauma cult, we don't even have an energy system at all. There is only mind and body, no such thing as the human spirit.

When a person has real PTSD, they have flashbacks to the causative trauma.

We don't need to dig for it, it's right there, and with any decent energy body focused therapy, can be successfully treated.

What we have now are people who are extremely stressed for many reasons, and they display some of the signs of real PTSD, but without the trauma flashbacks.

In order to explain how you can have PTSD without the causative trauma, we now have C PTSD, aka Complex Post Traumatic Stress Disorder, and we're back to general this-life-trauma, but lots and lots of it, and we're back to what we were already doing, which is to clear out all the trauma, and only then you'll feel better.

Let's stop once more and remember the millions of people who tried Past Life Regression in order to make progress and find evolution, alleviation of pain and symptoms, in their lives.

"This is it!" the people are crying right now, "Yes, I have Complex PTSD! I have all the symptoms – apart from the flashbacks, because there were too many traumas in my life! I am going to really focus on all the traumas, and then I'll be healed, and the sound of a door slamming will no longer cause me to have a panic attack!"

As C PTSD is comparatively new as an excuse as to why the previous trauma based therapy didn't work, I can't know how that will end up. I might predict that this will not alleviate the tsunami of mental health problems, diagnoses, and incredibly harmful prescription medications flooding our civilisations. I might indeed predict the exact opposite.

Every time you focus more on trauma, you will get more stress, more disturbances, more craziness across the board.

As people get more stressed, more trauma focus causes even more stress, until such time that something has to give, and there is a complete breakdown in the system.

The Medicalisation Of Mental Health

Psychology and trauma focused talking therapy never worked in the first place, especially not for people with real mental and emotional challenges such as soldiers returning from theatres of war.

There were many of those as the 2nd World War drew to a close; and this encouraged the idea that medication could be used to treat the people who were presenting with shell shock, battle fatigue or Post Traumatic Stress Disorder.

The psychiatrists, previously known as the psycho-medical doctors, wanted to use the physical model of medicine, by creating standardised diagnoses in order to prescribe standardised medications.

The original list of mental problems was drawn up in 1952, and contained 17 disorders, mostly based on the problems the returning soldiers were presenting with. This became the DSM (Diagnostic and Statistical Manual of Mental Disorders)[vii] published by the American Psychological Association, which has been expanded in the last 75 years to now contain nearly 300, none of which seem to have a successful treatment methodology associated with it.

There are, however, many forms of psychopharmaca prescriptions on offer instead.

A lady from New York says this about her clinical psychologist:

"Our monthly sessions were short. He kept his prescription pad in hand. He prescribed antidepressants; and antipsychotics to help with the antidepressants; and later, a course of amphetamines to help me concentrate – then sleeping pills for when it was time to come off of those."[viii]

A veteran says this about their experience:

"I saw the sign for Psychiatry as I walked down the hall. I remember it was just like a really small office and I was sitting in a chair and I said um sir every time I hear a door slam it sounds like a gunshot and my mind is racing like I need help. He said oh just take this medicine it'll make you feel better and I just picked up the prescription and started taking it. It was starting to make me worse but they just kept telling me that's what PTSD is, you have PTSD now and then I remember he looked at me and he said we're going to start the proceedings for medical retirement, you are not able to be around soldiers and no weapons and I remember feeling like how now I'm disabled at 25."[ix]

I could now go on to give you the latest statistics on the terrifying amounts of prescriptions for mental and emotional problems, about the side effects, about how many people are addicted to some kind of psychopharmaca; about the unfolding disaster that is called the opioid crisis, but that is not why we are here.

The proliferation of mental health diagnoses is now at a point where everyone in the therapy culture has some kind of syndrome, some kind of mental disorder.

The truth is that when people get stressed, they will show all the signs and symptoms of a mental disorder, and the more stressed they are, the worse this becomes.

This is perfectly predictable on the Modern Energy Chart.

We cannot begin to even know who is and who isn't mentally ill whilst everyone is so dangerously stressed all the time.

The pills can't cure that. Negative talking therapy, what remains of it, can't cure that, and it never could.

Within the trauma cult and the trauma therapy culture, there is literally no way out of this, not for the people who have suffered such severe trauma that they can no longer function, nor for everyone else who has simply succumbed to the incessant onslaught of negativity, fear mongering, the worsening or disconnection of their relationships with other people, the break down of law and order, the profound loss of trust in systems of authority, and the complete unpredictability of what madness is going to happen next – another plague, more totalitarian incarceration and removal of human rights, riots in the streets, nuclear holocaust, meteor strike or the entire world going up in flames due to climate change.

This truly is living in the fish tank of insanity.

Before we do anything else, we must first of all stabilise our frazzled, exhausted, overstressed energy systems, and that applies across the board, from every child to every youngster, every citizen and every veteran as well.

With every person who becomes de-stabilised, **all of society** becomes more and more de-stabilised.

In the absence of any workable or effective way to deal with all of that stress, which is a manifestation of the absence of love itself in the system, things can only get worse inside the trauma cult.

6: It's Perfectly Normal To Be An Emotional Wreck

Once upon a time, it was held that it was good to be happy.

It was good to be strong, positive, smiling, doing your work that you loved, building a present and a future for yourself and those you were responsible for.

Once upon a time, it was held to be a sign of mental instability to lose control of your emotions, to lose all sense of rhyme and reason, and throw yourself around like a proverbial lunatic.

Not so right here, right now, in 2024.

We can blame social media all we want; at the root of all of this is the trauma cult.

Apparently, we are all so traumatised by the terrible injustices and unfair treatments of our lives that it is not only perfectly normal to be an emotional wreck, it is desirable.

The more you scream and shout, the more power you gain over others; the more attention you get, the better a person you become.

It is fashionable now to have a mental illness diagnosis of some kind; it has become an advantage as things are getting more and more insane inside the trauma cult.

In the Western World, our current systems of government and justice are built around the idea that we have to be at least emotionally neutral to even be able to understand what is going on, or to be able to participate in such things as jury trials, or elect officials.

This is because in the Middle Ages, they already had worked out that stressed people will think and do really crazy things, and that's not good for anyone who is trying to maintain a civilised society.

Holding the line at Zero emotions is a tough gig in crazy times, but it is a baseline of societal operations that will hold a society together enough so it can function long term.

Please be advised that I am not advocating for having Zero emotions; I believe that we make the most of our systems at +10, and we should strive for as high as possible, to be as right as possible.

As you can imagine, people screaming and shouting about endless injustice and their trauma, is diametrically opposed to what I would want to see happening in any human, any human society; and I believe we got there by the trauma cult in the first place.

The Critical Theories
Or How To Ruin Anything Made Easy

Without going into the crazy nitty-gritty of the Critical Theories, as a short overview, we have the idea that the reason your life isn't working is because the system is rigged against you.

We then look for the trauma that the system has caused you, personally.

We start the process of negative journaling on the topic, until there is so much evidence of maltreatment and malfeasance that we get very, very angry.

We go out and find other people and add THEIR grievances to our own. This creates these so-called echo chambers, which amplify our righteous anger, ramps it up and up until we can't stand it any longer, we must bring out the pitchforks and torches, take to the streets and bring down the system with fire and sword.

We don't care what happens after that, and it doesn't matter anyway – the system is the enemy and only its complete destruction will end the pain.

That's the same process by which we end the pain and bring about the happy life by finding the one trauma that rules them all and when we take it out, heaven on Earth must ensue.

The interesting structure in the critical theories is that "the system" could be literally anything at all.

It could be a government, an opposing political party; it could be the school board, or the police; it could be the patriarchy, or the local water company.

"The System" could be a race of people, a group of people, one single representative of a group of people – literally, we can run the process of simply journaling all the negatives until we get so angry that we just want to smash it, on anything at all.

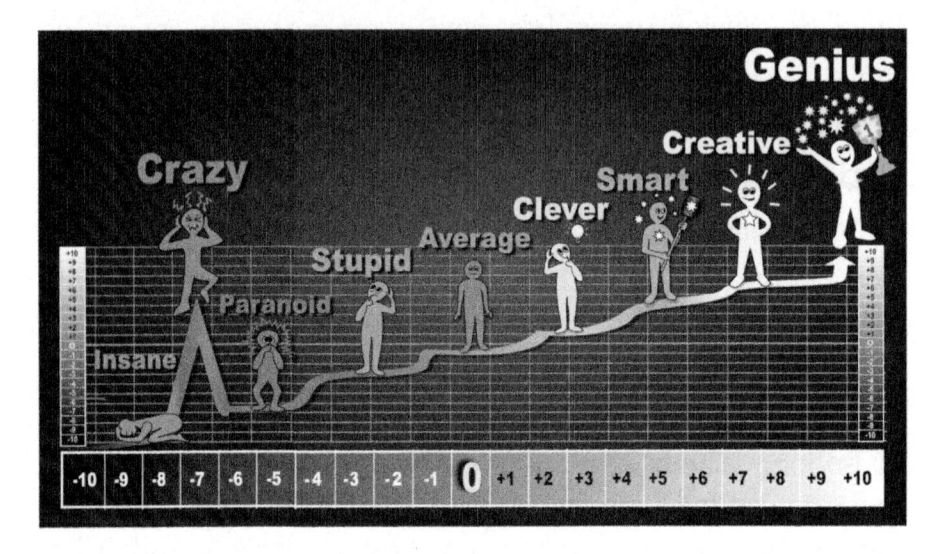

I have been showing people the Modern Energy Chart for years and explained to them that below -3, reason flies out of the door and whatever decisions any human being makes are going to turn out to be big mistakes in hindsight.

Our ability to calculate the repercussions of our activities collapses under stress and we naturally set events in motion that can be highly counter-productive.

For example, our local water company is severely mismanaged. Profits are sucked out by greedy investors, infrastructure is left to rot, there is corruption everywhere; the prices are too high and in the summer, in spite of it raining all the time as this is England, we have a ban on hose pipes and filling our kid's paddling pools.

If we spend a few months not only writing down all our own reasons to despise the water company, but get together with our neighbours and add all their negative experiences to our own, soon enough, we'll be on our way to the company with our torches and pitchforks, smash their computers, beat up the managers and set the headquarters on fire.

And now?

Now you turn on the tap, and there's no more water.

What now? I don't know how to fix that. The neighbours don't, either. The people who did know have fled in panic. Not being able to flush the toilets any longer may be alright for a day, but after that?

This is a simple example of how focusing on the trauma to the point that you get so angry, you want to smash the system is not a solution; it is not an evolution; and it isn't going to make anything better than it was before.

Yet, inside the cult of trauma, nobody realises this.

Nobody says, "Stop."

Nobody points out that trauma is teaching us what not to do, and how not to do it; but never how to create something, fix something, heal something, or bring about a better future.

Trauma ONLY Teaches Us What Not To Do

I realised a long time ago that trauma only teaches us what not to do.

This being so, it doesn't explain why we actually DO the things we actually DO.

Having been scared by a dog when we were kids explains perfectly why we avoid dogs.

It doesn't at all explain why we are now working as marine biologists.

It could be argued that we're focusing on the oceans and all the life that exists within them because there aren't any dogs in the oceans, but there are innumerable, infinite other places where we can spend our time and attention without the risk of ever meeting a dog.

Why didn't you become an astronaut instead?

"Well, there was that time my parents took me to a big aquarium and there was this small shark behind the glass and it looked at me ..."

It is fascinating what happens when people put two and two together about the actual life's choices they made, the things they DID, rather than endlessly focusing on what they don't do or don't want to do because of all that trauma.

It is also fascinating what happens when you start making it your business to inquire into why people do the things they do, rather than trying to dig up their trauma memories.

To understand that this person before us became an acclaimed marine biologist because of that event with the little shark when they were six years old tells us so much more about that person and their lives than any trauma story ever could.

This takes me to a whole realm of viewing other people not through the trauma lens for a change, and there is much I have to say on that topic.

For now, let's simply hold this thought in mind.

Trauma doesn't explain why you do the things you do.

It only explains the things you do not do.

That is true and you can rely on it. It's structural. It is an important building block in escaping the trauma cult but without throwing any babies out with the bathwater.

Trauma is real and it happens. What trauma isn't, is some gigantic Satan which we need to quiver before, in everlasting and never ending terror.

We need to reduce it in size and put it in its rightful place, and when we do that, we get all the other important life events back, the missing evidence which we needed all along to make some measure of sense of our own lives, and our true lived experience.

Lived Experience Doesn't Need To Be A Dirty Word

The concept of lived experience is very good in principle. We can read about many things in books or watch many things on screens, but that is not the same as having the experience, which teaches each one of us how things really are, in the really-real world.

However, when the trauma cult hijacks lived experience and reduces it to nothing but the insults, many very bad things happen all at the same time.

The worst factor in trauma fixation is the stress effect that precludes logical thinking.

When I say that it precludes logical thinking, I use that phrase as a metaphor which contains many important mental abilities inside.

The ability to connect cause and effect.

The ability to see patterns.

The ability to interpret patterns.

The ability to calculate potential outcomes.

These things are the tip of the iceberg when it comes to moving through actual reality with any degree of certainty and confidence.

Under stress, our personal event horizons shrink; our ability to think about the future collapses and at -7, it is gone completely.

When a person gets into the -7 stress states, they are 100% in the here and now, and can no longer even know that what they are about to do will bring about a death sentence in repercussion.

This really is a catastrophe, both for the person who is personally living this experience, as well as for the society, in which this person is supposed to function as a reliable member.

When many people enter into these stress states, get together and start making group decisions from such stress states, whatever they come up with, is 100% bound to be not only illogical in the full sense of all of the above, but guaranteed to result in extremely destructive models, systems and ideas.

This structure is not just how societies collapse, time and time anew; it is also the structure of what grows after those revolutions – insane, destructive systems that might take centuries to slowly spool up again to some kind of flourishing civilisation.

But what of the lived experience?

If you collapse the entirety of any person's lived experience to trauma only, and direct attention systematically to trauma only, then the lived experience of any person will be extremely traumatic. This is exacerbated when you collect groups of people who all add their negative lived experiences so that every person's trauma is shared by every other person in that group.

Now, lived experience has become weaponised and will be used to smash whatever gets in its way.

And all of that would change dramatically if we were to balance the books, finally create a fair trial, and take more evidence into consideration that does not just consist of trauma and more trauma, and nothing else, so help us God.

The Trauma Victims Race To The Bottom – And The Psychopaths Race To The Top

There is an interesting and very systemic process that happens when you put ten people into a room and have them tell each other their traumas.

A competition ensues as to whose trauma is the worst trauma.

This happens in group therapy as it happens anywhere else you bring people together to share their trauma based grievances.

The hierarchy of the group will be decided by who can produce the most impressive trauma.

Please note that I use the word "produce" rather than saying who experienced the worst trauma.

It isn't enough to have experienced trauma, to have those aforementioned lived experiences to draw upon. In the group setting, those who can PERFORM the most dramatic reconstructions, raise the most horrifying energy, will be the winners, and not necessarily the ones who have the most real lived experience of the relative trauma.

This opens the possibility that such groups end up being led by psychopaths, who have figured out how the game works, and now use the groups to their own benefit.

The lived experience of negative trauma, especially when it has been expanded to the lived experience trauma powerfield of an entire group, will literally overpower any argument based on logic and reason – or so it seems.

The Evil Scissors & The Trauma Cult

As mentioned before, Western civilisation is constructed around the idea that having no emotions is a safe place where we can hold the line and make somewhat rational decisions in a court of law, or do a somewhat rational version of science.

The very problem with that concept is that Zero Emotions have no energy, have no power; and worse, produce a reality-reduced version of logic and intelligence, because we find that only at +10.

Zero Emotions cannot stand up to the explosive anger of -7; this is how it comes to be that the rational Professor who is pleading for calm and reason is simply shouted down by a mob of angry students and has to flee in fear of their lives, being chased out of the building and down the road.

To hold the line in this situation, Zero doesn't cut the mustard. +8 is the minimum required to stand up to the onslaught of -7.

I would offer the metaphor of a sheriff in a small town, who has taken in a dangerous prisoner, and the town folks have worked each other up into the -7 mob state. They are marching on the prison now with their torches and pitchforks, but the sheriff stands on the doorstep and holds them off – not with a single pistol, but with their energy.

The sheriff gives an extraordinary speech, which is powered by their energy state, speaking the "magic words" as a direct result of being in this high energy state, and the town folks stop, then hang their heads in shame, turn around and walk away.

This is how it works. A single person can stand up to a -7 mob, but they need to be at +8 or above to accomplish this.

It is simple, logical, works in the real world with real people, but the trauma cult has done its best to take even the possibility that there could be anything other than trauma away – by essentially deleting the entire positive wing of the Modern Energy Chart from public consciousness.

I call that "The Evil Scissors[x]."

By not giving any attention to positive emotions, high positive emotions and the best, highest positive emotions, the anti-traumas, the Star Events, as I call them, the obvious way out of the trauma cult has been eradicated.

Now, we are left only with trauma, or nothing at all.

This creates *the fish tank of insanity*, where people are cycling round and round between being extraordinarily stressed, slowly spooling back up to Zero, which is nowhere near enough to escape the fishtank of insanity, then something else happens, attention is once more directed to some kind of trauma, real, imagined, someone else's trauma, back down to – 7, and so it goes, over and over again, in an ever tightening vicious spiral that destroys people's spirits, their intelligence, their health, their entire lives in the most extraordinary way.

As the trauma cult is in operation in all of the Western World, super charged thanks to psychology replacing the previous religions, this of course also destroys families, neighbourhoods, societies, science, culture, art and everything else that could be good and holy.

7: Microaggression, Triggers & Chronic Trauma Pain

The Western World suffers from chronic trauma pain, thanks to psychology, the reductionist materialistic paradigm of trying to explain the world with only five senses, and the underlying, inherited structure of "you have to descend to ascend."

There is another factor at play which I find fascinating, and unusually for me, this comes from the realms of physical medicine.

Here, we have many, many people who suffer from chronic pain that seems to have no medical cause. It is actually extraordinary just how many people go to their doctors and garner that diagnosis of "medically unexplained symptoms" or MUS.

In the current system, where there is no spirit, just mind and body, these patients get sent from the doctor to the psychologist, but the pain doesn't recede, so they go back to the doctor, who sends them back to the psychologist, and round and round it goes – another fishtank of insanity, where the patient who is trapped in that cycle gets ever more stressed, ever more desperate, ever more destabilised in their totality.

A medical doctor who treats these patients tells me that the constant focus by the patient on the pain signals creates ever stronger pathways in the neurology, and the more the patients focus on the pain, which is a perfectly natural thing to do, the stronger the pain signals get, and the more sensitised the patient becomes over time.

As there are no pills or any other types of mechanical or physical interventions that work to help these patients, this doctor teaches them to focus on different parts of their body in order to build different pathways.

I suggested that it would work to teach those patients to draw a spiral in the palm of their hand as a place of focus, but as we were chatting about this, I was of course thinking how the trauma victims do exactly the same thing.

After an entire lifetime being totally immersed in the trauma cult, and being trained all the way and every day to focus only on trauma as the explanation for everything, joining up in echo chambers where trauma is shared, bred, multiplied, what pathways have been built here, what train tracks in the physical brain?

We may well wonder …

What I want us to take away from this is the understanding that what we focus our attention on will become highlighted; and over time, will make us not only experience more and more pain, but it will also make us much more sensitive than we were before, and get triggered into pain experiences quicker, easier, and more profoundly.

What we have here is the structural explanation for the emergence of "microaggression" in the Western World.

Mobile Phones Murder Meaningful Connections

In 2012, I became so worried about the state of the populations in the Anglosphere, that I created the first direct Modern Stress Management program, which explains the Modern Energy Chart, and most importantly, teaches ways to raise energy to become stronger, smarter and healthier.

There is no doubt in my mind that the huge jump in stress in the population is directly linked to the onset of mobile phone usage.

I look at this from the energy-inclusive perspective, and if you do that, it becomes immediately obvious what the core problems are.

The most profound problem with mobile phones is that they get in the way of natural human interaction in the real world.

Human beings have real living energy bodies, and these are designed to exchange energy with other human beings.

There is a process by which two people get together, and synchronise with each other; their energy systems come into alignment and they create what I call a couple bubble.

Once this couple bubble is established, people laugh together; easily share ideas with each other and feel positive emotions. That's the feedback that their energy system is happier than it was before; they have done something good and they know it.

When mobile phones came in, that natural process of harmonisation and connecting with another person in the same room became severely disrupted.

"I'm sorry, I have to take this ..."

Five minutes later:

"What were you saying?"

People were spending time together, perhaps even as much time as before, but that synchronisation wasn't happening; it was being disrupted and put right back to the beginning, time and time again.

The deep connective, extremely important and nourishing energy connections weren't happening any longer, and that is a huge, huge problem among adults.

I also observed that children were getting even less attention than they ever had, because their parents were always being distracted by their mobile phones, or would even choose their mobile phones over their small children.

Children need attention. They need copious amounts of attention, and attention is energy, energy is real, it's LOVE, and when children don't get that when they grow up, it leaves them stressed, and therefore much more likely to develop all manner of problems across mind, body and spirit.

These are the very fundamental basics of the damage mobile phones have done to human interactions; but of course, there's so much more.

Endless streams of stress crazy and stress inducing micro-injections into the human totality, all day long, all the time, and it doesn't stop, ever.

Have you noticed that when you are scrolling through a social media feed, and someone has posted a particularly nasty picture of some horrid food, that your stomach turns over?

And that picture of the nasty food is just one out of how many million you have seen – and your totality REACTED to every image in some way, a clenching up here, a firing of something there, an emotion, an energy sensation, a thought …

It's incalculable what we have done to our totalities by doing this, for years on end.

What is easily calculable however is how much more stressed the population has become.

And now we are in real trouble in the trauma cult, because the question of "Why are we so stressed?" can have only one single answer: It's because we've been traumatised!

You are questioning reality? Must be because of a childhood trauma with your father.

You are anxious? Tell me about the trauma …

You are paranoid? What trauma caused this?

You are angry? You must have been soooo traumatised by all those terrible things that were done to you?

Whose fault is this?

Where are the perpetrators?

We can also go a step back and diagnose all the symptoms of stress as actual mental illnesses.

This is a great move on the part of the trauma cult.

If someone "has" a mental disorder, then it can't ever be fixed, or expected to be fixed.

That is a great relief for those who are theoretically supposed to find ways to help people with their symptoms, but have no way to do that in the first place.

If you have ADHD, that's it then. That's the explanation for your symptoms, and now you can go on, happily ever after, with your ADHD, never get better, never expect to get better, and the system runs beautifully.

I have to say that I could weep every single time I come across a person who is so, so joyous that they "finally know what's wrong with me – I have ADHD!" or whatever it is that they have been diagnosed with. Clearly, any diagnosis that explains what's going on is going to produce that happy response – but you know what? I predict if you check on their happiness status for more than two weeks, we might just find that this initial apparent gain has flattened out, and their lives aren't any happier at all, nor have their symptoms receded in any meaningful way.

The fact is that every normal human being, when they become stressed enough, will reliably produce all the symptoms of real mental illness.

I have said for a long time that we need to de-stress people first of all.

When we do that, we take out all the normal people who have absolutely nothing wrong with them, apart from the fact that some kind of stress has literally driven them crazy. What we are left with then is the people who really do have a mental illness, and now we can study those and learn something significant.

We need to re-do every experiment, every research study, ever, in both psychology and medicine, and account for the stress levels of the participants. Then we might learn something that is of use downstream, for the general population.

Returning to the highly stressed population, whose stress was directly exacerbated by the onset of mobile phones, and who had been pre-programmed to filter for trauma and grievances, the question arose how to avoid the pain of negative emotions.

How do you not have negative emotions?

Why, if your trauma wasn't triggered, you could live happily ever after.

Welcome to political correctness.

Political Correctness

The first incident I directly remember was some people deciding they were triggered by Father Christmas and the general Christianity of Christmas itself, and the campaign to stop saying, "Merry Christmas!" in order to not trigger those who were triggered by Christmas, or Christians.

What surprised me was that instead of telling these people to work on their triggers so they wouldn't be triggered anymore and could join in the festivities, the place where this happened essentially banned Christmas.

I remember clearly thinking, "If we were to ban everything that triggers anyone, there wouldn't be much left ..."

I have been watching how this has unfolded over the last 25 years and I am still thinking that.

Of course, it has gotten much, much worse.

Focusing on the insults, focusing on the trauma, in addition to all the high stress already in society, has brought us to ever more sensitised, ever more stressed people who are now abreacting to microaggressions.

The rest of the population is completely bemused by this, has no idea what is happening to their societies, to their families, and are getting ever more stressed in turn.

The divisiveness which results from this is also frightening, although predictable.

In the meantime, the trauma cult has no way of fixing this; in fact, it is the very cause of this destruction.

A Few Statistics

One in five children and young people in England aged 8 to 25 had a probable mental disorder in 2023. The Mental Health of Children and Young People in England 2023 report, published by NHS England, found that 20.3% of eight to 16-year-olds had a probable mental disorder in 2023. Among 17 to 19-year-olds, the proportion was 23.3%, while in 20 to 25-year-olds it was 21.7%.[4]

80% of college students say they are struggling emotionally, 20% saying they are struggling significantly. 58% say they are dealing with declining mental and emotional health. Students are largely dealing with anxiety (59%) and burnout (58%), followed by depression (43%).[5]

Following the Pandemic, parents of children under the age of 18 were more likely to report that on most days their stress is completely overwhelming (48% vs. 26%), they are so stressed they feel numb (42% vs. 22%) or on most days they are so stressed they can't function (41% vs. 20%).[6]

Can we now please finally agree and declare Psychology a failed pseudo science?

Have we assembled enough lived experience yet to clearly state that trauma driven psychology does not work, can not work, does not explain people, and in fact, mistreats people by keeping them locked in that fish tank of insanity, where there is no such thing as positive

---

[4] https://www.england.nhs.uk/2023/11/
[5] College Students US CA Wiley Survey November 2023
[6] November 2023 Stress in America™ A nation grappling with psychological impacts of collective trauma

emotions, no hope of healing or of evolution, and certainly, woven throughout, that appalling lack of love itself?

Can we?

Can we point to the psychology emperor and say, "You have no clothes on. Your theories are ridiculous, your methods non-existent, your results beyond pathetic?"

I would like to do that, right now.

End the nightmare of trauma.

End the rule of the reductionist materialistic five sense paradigm.

Do it now, or we will be standing in the ruins of societies that took a long time and a lot of effort to build, to get us to a place where we are no longer starving physically – but where through the lack of love itself we created a concentration camp for our very spirits.

8: Escaping The Fish Tank Of Insanity

Whilst I was looking for entries for the "A few statistics" chapter, I came across this.

Stress in America™ 2023, a nationwide survey conducted by The Harris Poll on behalf of the American Psychological Association APA among more than 3,000 U.S. adults age 18+.

Nearly a quarter of adults (24%) rated their average stress between eight and 10 on a scale of one to 10 where one means little to no stress and 10 means a great deal of stress.

I would like to draw your attention to the scale they were using for this poll.

The scale goes from Zero Stress to Ten Stress.

There isn't any not-stress on this scale; there isn't any joy, any happiness, any LOVE at all; the positive wing of the Modern Energy Chart is yet again, absent.

I cannot overestimate the enormity of the problem with the conceptual absence of the happy emotions.

Science loves to reduce reality to controllable variables you can duplicate in the test scenario, in a laboratory, or in running computer simulations.

Reducing the complexity of something that happens to be complex in nature leads to a reality reduction, and that in turn leads to a huge problem which I like to call a "reality divergence."

A reality divergence is when people believe one thing, but it's not true.

For example, someone might believe that the sun is shining, but in fact, it is raining.

This naturally leads to the person becoming cold and wet, as they have taken no precautions against the rain.

Now we have a reality divergence. We cannot explain any longer how we came to be wet; it's very mysterious indeed.

As human beings, we try to make sense of our environments; and we have the capacity to come up with all manner of explanations as to why a person would get soaked, freezing cold, when it's a lovely day and the sun is shining brightly.

When a reality divergence occurs, life becomes stressful; more and more stressful, the longer it goes on, and the more reality diverged the people become.

I think of this as a rubber band that is being stretched and stretched and stretched – eventually, it will break and snap back into actual reality in a catastrophic fashion.

In actual reality, and there really is such a thing, people do not just have negative emotions.

To reduce a measuring instrument of emotions that is missing half the scale is a reality divergence; we have reduced the model so much, it no longer either reflects reality, or works in reality.

The missing positive wing of the Modern Energy Chart, which maps major emotion states, aka energy body states, holds literally everything that is important, that is precious, and above all else, that is true.

It is my assertion that the closest any human being can get to understanding reality absolute is when they are in the highest possible energy state for that individual – at +10.

I am not convinced we can live there; I believe that normal human beings go up and down on the entire Modern Energy Chart, and that all of that is a part of the experience of being human.

I do know however, that by taking away the entire positive wing of the scale we lose the GOAL – to be as high as possible, as often as possible.

We lose the way out of the fishtank of insanity, and I suspect that is why it was constructed, why all the measurements end at Zero, and why it has been so effective in trapping people within it.

Misdirecting attention to the worst energy states, the -7 moments, has directly created not just the fish tank of insanity, but also the hypersensitization to triggers and the inability of people who have been way too highly stressed all their lives to have any control over their emotions.

The focus on trauma has driven us collectively, societally, crazy.

Psychology Stole The Hope Of Healing

Decades ago, I became aware of the fact that psychology doesn't have a healed state for bereavement.

I am sure that you've heard of the 7 stages of bereavement; what is missing is the 8th stage, when the pain of bereavement has not just gone, but the loved one is present, and a source of profound strength, inspiration and support – the healed state of bereavement, which I call "The Immortal Beloved[7]," is completely absent, even as a concept.

The very idea that a person could ever be healed of their problems isn't there.

We find the same thing with soldiers who are told that they now "have" PTSD, or the children who "have" ADHD and therefore, need to stay on their medications for the rest of their lives. There isn't even the hope of a healed state here, and if you stop and think about it for a moment, what does it do to a person to live life without hope that it could ever get any better?

Recently, I saw an article with the title that "Forgiveness Is Bad For Survivors Of Child Abuse." Forgiveness is something that happens naturally when the emotional pain has gone, has been healed, and when that happens, and it doesn't hurt any longer, the person moves naturally and normally into the forgiveness states with their unique, positive and beneficial emotions.

---

[7] The immortal Beloved Modern Energy Based Bereavement Healing Protocol, Silvia Hartmann 2023

In the Trauma Cult, however, you get to stay a "survivor" forever; you will never be healed; there is no such thing as a healed state, and now we make out that the very idea of forgiveness is actually bad for you, and we shouldn't even seek it.

"We have literally no idea how to treat you, how to help you" has metastasized into the outright lie that you can't be healed, that it is impossible, and you should give up trying to find healing, give up all hope.

Every time any person gets one of these multi-letter "diagnoses" with the prescription of the day inside the trauma cult, something truly terrible has happened to their spirit. But it doesn't end there.

Why The Trauma Cult Destroys The Most Important Relationships

The most fundamentally important relationship in any person's life is that with their father and mother.

I do not know when it was that I read in a list of "How To Identify A Cult" the entry about how cults break up the relationships the person had with their family.

Of course, there's brothers and sisters, aunts and uncles, grandparents and all that, but the primary focus of cults is to destroy the relationship between a person, and their father and mother, because that will also destroy the relationship with whatever societal matrix father and mother operate within at the same time.

All cults are good at this and they have their various means and methods to accomplish this; the trauma cult of psychology tops them all.

There is a tendency among young human adults during their teenage years to start to complain to each other about how terrible their parents are, stopping them from having fun, forcing them to work, interfering in their social connections, holding old fashioned views, and on and on.

You don't see this in younger children; but teenagers do it naturally.

You hitch your star to that wagon and really direct the young adults' attention on everything mother and father ever did wrong or failed to do, and you absolutely will sever the original relationship, destroy the original relationship.

Let us be sure to note that this doesn't just happen when a young adult in the Western world enters into therapy; it is being prescribed all around in tropes in every modality, constantly reinforced, and that's what cults like to do.

Breaking up relationships has recently taken another massive threshold shift with the introduction of the idea that some people are horrible narcissists.

This is yet another mental health diagnosis that is being flung around like so much manure with a strong fan behind it, and the symptoms of having a narcissistic parent, or partner, are likewise to be found if we stare blindly through the trauma lens, and negatively journal every little indication of a real human being acting selfishly, wanting to get their way, looking out for themselves.

The fact is that when we are stressed, low on energy, we will naturally engage in selfish actions.

There is a direct correlation between a person's energy average, and how emotionally disconnected they become, as well as how selfish they appear to be. This is a natural self preservation process; so we can say clearly that anybody at all who becomes too stressed will show the 15 signs of being a narcissist, predictably, reliably, measurably.

However, once we start labelling and dehumanising a person as "a narcissist," we are once more breaking those all important real energetic connections through which energy, attention and love can flow. Predictably, this will destroy the relationship; and that's what the cult wants. No relationship with the family, no relationship with the partner, and all that remains is the cult and the other followers.

I personally am trying to create a Matrix that helps people be less stressed, that works with the nature of people and not against it, and a part of that is to have strong, real, life giving energy connections with the people in a person's life.

Our energy bodies need to be fed by the energy of other people. There are different types of energy connections and different types of energy flows; but the most crucially important of all of them are that primary relationship between a person, and their mother and father.

When this relationship is strong and works, everyone is happier, stronger and healthier.

When it doesn't, everyone suffers.

Everyone becomes stressed.

Stressed behaviours result which include the endless search for a replacement energy. The therapist becomes mother and father instead; the cult becomes the family.

This is unnatural, unhealthy, and doesn't benefit anyone at all.

Please note I just said, "It doesn't benefit anyone at all."

We may say, "Oh, it benefits the therapists, they're making lots of money from the endless circuits round and round the various fish tanks of insanity!"

If you count the best life only in terms of how much money a person gets to make, you might think that. I'm pretty sure there are plenty of statistics about burn out and suicide in the psychology "community," and I am sorry.

I am going to restate this one more time:

The unnatural, unhealthy trauma cult doesn't benefit anyone at all.

It is a reality divergence, and as with all reality divergences, sooner or later, we pay the price when the catastrophic snap back of the overstretched rubber band occurs, and real reality shows us the error of our ways.

Having good relationships, which are in fact real energy connections between our own living energy bodies and theirs, is of the essence for human health and happiness.

It is also of the essence for human intelligence, logic, and the ability to create systems that aren't as damaging and reality reduced as what we have had to deal with in the past.

The very first step to escaping the trauma cult is to reinstate the positive wing of the Modern Energy Chart.

Bring Back The Positive Emotions!

If you have come this far, I must presume that at least some of the things I have said have resonated with you.

I am now going to ask you to take a fresh look at the world, and notice that people may well be stressed and going crazy, as is to be expected under the circumstances; but I want you to now also notice that people are still sometimes happy, sometimes successful, sometimes in love, and that they smile sometimes.

You do too.

You might do this far more often than you think, especially if you have spent an absolute lifetime only focusing on what's wrong with everything, and that's OK.

Once we widen out our conception to include not just the negative side of everything, but also the positive side, we start a process of letting in more information; and information and energy are interchangeable.

This is something I have found fascinating. When we work with someone's energy system directly, through EMO Energy in Motion[xi] for example, and there's some kind of blockage that releases, it is always accompanied by a rush of information at the same time.

People cry out, "OMG, now I understand!" as they connect up various experiences, insights and pieces of information that seemed disconnected, but now make sense.

The more information we have, the better.

And please let me explain, when I say "information" I don't mean second-hand information that comes from written texts or other people; I am talking about information about reality absolute.

Lived experience.

Our lived experience needs to tally with the systems of information we are using to think about them, make sense of them.

If it doesn't, bad things happen in mind, body and spirit. Stress ensues and as you know by now, once we human beings get too stressed, insanity, chaos and destruction follow as truly as night follows day.

Lived experience is all we have, at the end of the day.

It is our personal truth, and that is true.

However, it is only when we stop thinking of our lived experience and our personal truth in terms of nothing but trauma that we truly and finally escape the fish tank of insanity and enter into a very different world, where hope, happiness and love are so much more than just simple words.

9: A Matrix Built Of Stars

Right at the beginning I said that I became aware that I was engaged in building a Matrix from the ground up, following my breakthrough experience with the invisible something, that turned out to be energy, that turned out to be love.

I said that I was nervous about that, uncomfortable with such a task. I had never asked to be put in a position where I would be tasked with such a thing; and what I did not want to do was to build yet another Matrix that sounds great to start with, creates those early initial gains, then flattens out and turns destructive in the end.

There were some components, however, which held my developing Matrix in place.

The first component was obviously not just the presence of LOVE as an absolute reality, but the fact that the entire Matrix was built on love in the first place.

Love is the most fundamental, most powerful force in the Universe.

When love is present, everything changes; miracles occur.

When love is absent, bad things start to happen, and this is predictable, measurable, and gets ever worse, the less love there is.

This is the core of my Matrix, and this is what I would come back to when I got stressed, scared about that whole business of building a new Matrix.

Reconnecting with this essential core, which was my lived experience and personal truth, stabilised me and allowed me to go forward.

I know this now; this is the truth, now how can I explain this to the people in my world who are completely immersed in a world that only recognises 5 senses, and who isn't really talking about love any longer?

I could get a megaphone and start shouting in the streets, or from the rooftops, about love.

I could hire advertising people who could make a clever marketing campaign.

I could do that whole cult leader trip, that's easy enough.

I watched so, so many people who did these things, and how they developed their often extremely enthusiastic followers, but I just did not want to build that kind of Matrix yet again.

I wanted a better one, one that is much more respectable of the human spirit, but also of all the human systems, the human totality, which is beyond amazing and doesn't get the credit it deserves, nor the love.

Finally, in 2019, the problems that I had with all the old cults were resolved and the way forward became clear, at last – the only way to free the people and bring them back to their own intelligence, their own power and their own, natural, inherent spirituality was through their own lived experience.

What was needed was to redirect their attention from the worst moments of their lives, to the best moments of their lives instead.

Instead of telling them how to feel or even what to think, we can simply ask people about the best moments of their lives, the Star Moments, and what they learned from that.

This creates a completely different experience for not only the client, but for the therapist as well; it creates a space where love itself can manifest, can be known, can be discussed and absolutely will empower everyone who engages in this activity.

As we have noted before, it is only once you have escaped from a destructive Matrix, from the trauma cult, do you really understand how much is lost when we operate from the wrong core principles.

We had literally no idea of what extraordinary "magic" can be created between two people in a therapy setting when we switch from focusing on trauma to focusing on the Star Events; nor how this simple switch highlighted the endless shortcomings and destructive practices deemed so normal handed down by the trauma cult.

Let's have a look at a few examples.

10,000 Hours In Therapy

A famous professor of clinical psychology said in 2024 during an interview, and I quote, "The disenfranchised need 10,000 hours in therapy, maybe more, before they feel they are being heard and can establish real lines of communication with the therapist."

My young aspects had heard of people being in therapy for decades, three times a week for 45 years with the same therapist (there was a news report of such a pairing, where the client died, and the therapist died the week after that). She could never understand how such a thing could come to be - but didn't enquire into it any further.

However, during the psychology-based trauma EFT Tapping time, what was happening in therapy at large began to reveal itself.

Negative EFT Tapping requires for the practitioner to listen to what the client is saying, and from all those words to pick out one single statement to tap on. Depending on how well the therapist could do that, the session would become very emotional and worth the money to the client.

Within a few month of doing this with clients and in demonstrations every day, my aspect noticed that the clients would come into any session in quite severe stress states, -3 at the best and vibrating with anxiety at -6 more often, and if you asked them what their problem was, they would launch into what my aspect came to think of as "a flood of meaningless stress talk" - long incoherent sentences, skipping from one thing to the other, like a printed page in all CAPS with no line breaks, or even punctuation.

This made it obviously very difficult to pick out one thing from this flood to get the trauma tapping party started; but as time went by, my aspects noted a much greater problem with this stress talk.

This problem was that the client wasn't actually telling me what their real problems were.

You could say that a highly stressed person is structurally incapable of even knowing what their real problems are, and neither could they express this in words, even if they did know.

The answer to this problem was to not allow the client to go into stress talk the moment they had sat down on the therapy couch, but instead, to stabilise them with the Heart Position and bringing in a little energy first, to bring the client to at least +3 before we even ask what the problem may be.

This resulted in much more coherent clients; the Opening Statements/Set Ups could be more easily agreed on; and as we were now dealing with real problems rather than a flood of stress grievances about literally everything that was wrong with the client's life, the sessions would be much, much more helpful.

In the trauma cult, we do not have the Modern Energy Chart; and if we did, it wouldn't have the positive wing, or even the idea that we want to move the client up and into the Positives, so we as the therapists get to have an equal, intelligent partner in the investigation of whatever the problem may be.

What we do have, thanks to the stress talk factor, is a situation if where you get your client in and just let them stress talk for 45 minutes about their current problems with the world and its wife, you can do the same thing next week, and the week after that, and the week after that, and soon enough, you have your 10,000 hours in therapy.

It's a perfect system to keep both clients and therapists on a hamster wheel, or nicely trapped in the fish tank of insanity forever.

This pattern, however, sadly is not confined to therapists and their clients in the Western World. It has become the go-to way of behaving and interacting with friends and family as well – stress talk all the way, and nobody calls to put a STOP to it, because nobody knows that this is a destructive and counterproductive way of societal interaction.

It seems normal, it seems "natural" in the trauma cult to start any conversation, any social media post with this stress talk that is always focused on insults, grievances, negative events and occurrences – because that's what happens in a cult. The weirdest things seem normal, natural, when they are not.

It doesn't have to be that way.

Armed with the Modern Energy Chart, we can simply say that when a person is below Zero, there is little point in even listening to what they have to say.

"Stress talk isn't worth the paper it isn't written on."

The problem here is that not only do people not know that stress talk is completely counterproductive; to sort for the insults, all the time, has created true train tracks in the brain that function like the chronic pain paths, so as time goes by, things are going to become ever worse.

How Do You Stop All The Negativity?

Moving people up the Modern Energy Chart before we even begin to ask the question, "What's the problem here?" was only the first tentative step on the path from the darkness to the light.

It is amazing to me that I didn't see it earlier that trauma itself was the problem; I was still operating under the rules of the cult, where trauma is all and everything, and if only we could get rid of it, we could live happily ever after ...

But I didn't see it at the time.

What I did see was that the people who were using what I called Energy EFT at that time (to make sure we all know, therapists AND clients alike, that we were working with ENERGY!), weren't using it at all to its full potential.

You have the Modern Energy Chart.

You have identified some kind of trauma block for the problem, let's say, "Mummy never loved me."

You do the Energy Tapping with the client, and stop every so often to ask where they are now on the Modern Energy Chart.

After a few sequences, the client says, "I feel much better. +5, yay!" and the therapist would stop the session there and let them go home.

Now the thing with energy treatments is that to be complete, you need a +10 experience, a true healing event, where the client's problem has evolved, will never come back in its original form, and the client is dancing with joy.

Yet the therapists didn't take that final step, to ask, "What do we need now to completely transform this?" and they did not finish the session properly.

This annoyed me so much, I decided to take the whole trauma thing away, and switch to positive solutions instead.

Instead of starting by stating the problem, trying to find a causative trauma, and laboriously tapping with the client on some hugely painful experience to crawl up the Modern Energy Chart, I switched to the Power of the Positives and what is essential Art Solutions.

"Don't paint the problem – paint the solution!"

What is the problem?

"My mother never loved me."

What do you need to get over that?

"The love of God itself."

We tap on the solution, and the +10 will come, quickly and profoundly as we keep asking, "And what else do you need …?"

It could not be any easier if you tried – but by taking away the trauma digging, we were now outside the cult of psychology altogether, and that was the point in 2011[xii] at which I moved Modern Energy into the Third Field in the Mind, Body, Spirit triad and unfolded my new Matrix there instead, where it rightfully belonged.

We Are Not Doing Psychology, We Are Doing Modern Energy

Now, we have a serious problem.

We are now dealing with a field that has neither decent theories nor decent practices; and we are dealing with the entire population who are all brainwashed to believe that they only have five senses, and no spirit at all.

There are some people who believe in energy, but because there isn't a stable Matrix, just strange constructions wonkily cobbled together from an array of incompatible "ancient traditions," blatant nonsense and all sorts of the whispers of the ages, even these people are confused and uncertain; they often know things and feel things but lack the ability to express themselves clearly.

Of course, there are also the usual grifters which can be found in any field of human endeavour, who lie, cheat and steal to amass money and worldly power; and the more stressed the population becomes, the more such grifters take their chances to make their buck.

People are confused, stressed and suspicious. It is extremely difficult to be heard, although the Modern Energy Chart has helped enormously with its simple clarity and observability in lived experience.

In our beginner's trainings, I like to start now with the words,

"What is the most important part of you that has received the least amount of attention?"

This always causes a chuckle in the audience; but the answer, **"Your own real living energy body!"** is a lovely foundation to get started.

Over the years, and by focusing on the question, "What makes the energy body happy?" I have developed a treasure chest of techniques and base patterns that will accomplish that. It will make the energy body happier, and when that is happier, the owner of said energy body will be happier too. Cause and effect, dear friends …

However, if all we ever do is chase the elusive trauma so we can finally live happily ever after, and that is actually the wrong thing to be chasing in the first place, it doesn't matter how wonderful the techniques and methods might be we are employing.

It doesn't matter if we are armed with a rock, bow and arrow, a gun or a lightsabre when we're chasing an illusionary monster that doesn't exist across the moors.

Until and unless we stop doing that, taking a moment to breathe deeply and look around for what else there might be, nothing can change.

The most important step to free ourselves from the trauma cult is to come home to the actual reality of our lives, and end the trauma-centric reality divergence that is driving us all insane.

Breaking The Trauma Curse: The Timeline Of Events

In 1993, I saw the reality of love as being a major causative factor in not just animal behaviour, but in human behaviour too.

In 2000, I found the Guiding Stars, those half positive events that cause looping behaviour as they try endlessly to complete themselves, and which are the cause for addictions, fetishes and philias.

By 2008, I had found other types of events, actual events in the energy system that caused permanent changes to that person, and I would encourage people to consider the following short meditation.

Imagine a starry space, and in this space, there is your life line, from the moment of your conception to right here and now.

Put all your traumas on this life line, little red flashing lights.

This is your trauma line, and sadly, for a lot of people that is all there is.

But this isn't the whole story, or the real story.

Let's add some little green lights to this life line, and the green lights stand for all the events where something was healed, something was learned, something was understood – let's call them the Healing Events. As you consider this enriched life line now, notice that it feels a little bit better, like a relief, a tension released.

Now we'll add some turquoise lights. These are for strange and mysterious events you have experienced, and we can't quite know whether they were good, or bad, or even what they were – the Unknowable Events.

Your life line is starting to become a little more interesting ...

Our next lights are purple, and those stand for the Missing Events, energy system events we should have had, but they never happened.

And finally, let's add some bright white stars that really sparkle – those are your Star Events, the best moments of your life.

Now, doesn't that life line make a lot more sense? Do you feel a lot better, considering your life with simply more and different events, and not only trauma?

I didn't know it then, but this was such an important step towards a much more realistic overview of any person's life. The fact that people say, "Yes, I feel much calmer, and strangely more hopeful after doing this meditation, perhaps even a little excited ..." told me then that I was on the right track with the idea that we have to reduce the trauma obsession before we can make any progress.

This was all good and well, but still, it was not enough to break the vast majority out of that appalling prison of the trauma cult.

I didn't give up. I kept working with the Power of the Positives[xiii] – the Power of Love itself, especially during the global panic pandemic, to keep our spirits up and find a way to take us higher.

The problem how to make a person feel better through Modern Energy Techniques had been solved decades ago; the new mission was to try and find a way to raise the energy average permanently, so that we wouldn't constantly have to be applying techniques and methods to rescue ourselves from the negative stress states, but instead, could get on with living our lives and having fun instead.

The energy AVERAGE is hugely important in the greater scheme of things.

The living energy body has a self healing function, which is disabled below Zero. How effective this self healing can be is determined by how often this self healing function has the energy to do some self healing, and this is the connection between time and healing.

In essence, the higher a person's energy AVERAGE, the quicker time will heal whatever energy problems they have accumulated in the past.

In other words, when you are reasonably energy high, your past traumas will be automatically healed, and you don't have to apply any methods to make that happen.

Not only that, your energy problems will be healed in the correct order and sequence, and that includes healing repressed trauma we don't even know we carry.

We don't have to dig for it; we don't need hypnosis to find it; it will be healed by the energy body itself if we give it enough resources to do its natural job, the job it was designed to do in the first place.

The self healing energy body demands that we raise our energy average – and how to do that was my next big research project from 2010 onward.

And finally, a quarter of a century after starting on this epic mission to bring love back into the worlds of thinking modern human beings, it happened – I understood how we can do it, how we can de-program the victims of the trauma cult, without dragging them straight into the next destructive Matrix.

And if you think about, and of course, I do, and have done, non-stop for decades, it is the sheer obviousness of the great discovery that is so telling.

8 Billion Prophets

If we look across the history of humanity, as well as how things are right, right now, we will notice that there are some people who become "cult leaders." They have an idea, the idea is popular, and they amass their followers.

The followers can be whipped up into all manner of strange activities, destructive, counterproductive, loveless modes of being and doing, and all manner of personal and societal madness ensues.

There is a scene in a humorous movie where the cult leader stands in a high place and shouts at their followers, "I want you to think for yourselves!" and the assembled crowd shouts back, "We think for ourselves!"

The way all these cult matrices of the past operated was not what I wanted. Born in Germany after the 2nd World War, the idea of having endless blocks of ant people repeating my words and shouting my name wasn't ever where I wanted to be.

There is, however, a different way.

When very energy high individuals come together, a different kind of group emerges. This has been described as a "mastermind group" in the past; these are individuals who know who they are, have a strong sense of self, and do not dissolve when their energy systems align with each other.

Rather, what happens here is that they begin to experience a form of expanded thinking, where each one becomes more than the sum of their parts.

However, for this to be even possible, the individuals entering into this extraordinary yet entirely human experience must be stable within themselves, and very energy high.

What we need to make significant changes for humanity is to have these energy high groups of people work on whatever problems they are attempting to solve – instead of a single prophet here and there leading their little flock of sheep, we need 8 billion prophets, all at the same time, everywhere on Earth.

Now, with the Modern Energy Chart, and all the many assembled techniques to raise energy, we were closer to this idea of more stable, much energy higher people working together for the good of humanity, which in and of itself is a meaningful goal to work towards.

As I was contemplating these things, and trying to figure out how we could possibly get there, when everyone is so stressed, everyone is so traumatised, everyone is such an emotional mess, thinks of themselves as eternal victims to all manner of invisible and malignant forces that are entirely out of their control, I still did not consciously realise that I was myself still trapped inside the trauma cult – and of course, if you think of the people of planet Earth like that, there is no possible solution to the endless problems of humanity.

Yet all along and all the time, I could see the light within; I did know that people were not what they thought they were, not at all, but I didn't know how I could show it to them, or tell them, and even if I did, of course they would not believe me.

After all I had seen, experienced and been through, I was still nervous to even start a research project on the high positive memories, Project 11, in 2019.

I "sold it" to the participants by saying, "Let's take a trauma holiday. Let's take a holiday from all that endless healing that we all think we need. We've been doing that for such a long time now, let's do something different for a change."

Of course I knew that interacting with high positive memories, the Star Events, would be fun. I knew it would raise energy. I knew we would discover some wonderful things that we would never, ever discover by working with more injuries and more trauma.

But I admit absolutely that I had no idea at all of the power of our own Star Memories to take us finally out of the trauma cult, to free us from the fish tank of insanity for good, and show us the way to a radically new and different way, not only for therapy and healing, but how to deal with life itself.

It was in the engagement with my own Star Memories that I finally escaped the trauma cult.

It was when I realised that I was not the broken, beaten, traumatised, neglected, poor, victim child that I had believed myself to be my whole life long - I was the blessed child instead.

I had assembled so much evidence over the course of a year and a half of working with my own Star Memories that I was no longer a victim and I was finally freed from the trauma cult - and you can be too, if you want to.

10: Star Matrix Is The Way

Remember the bright white sparkling stars on our time line which contains all our life's events?

The Star Memories. The best moments of our lives. The ONLY memories that flash before our eyes as our plane ditches towards the ocean ...

The sheer obviousness of this is so breathtaking, and it absolutely reveals the enormity of the brainwashing we all received from the trauma cult.

The most important moments in a person's life have been not only completely overlooked in psychology research, they have been edited out of conscious awareness.

They disappeared the moment the evil scissors went into action, and all the positive emotions were removed from public discourse and consciousness.

The most important moments of enlightenment, of intelligence, of understanding, of transformation, of evolution – all gone.

Only the ashes of trauma remained.

Yes, I am angry.

Angry at myself for taking so long to understand, taking so long to free myself from the all encompassing cult of trauma, and so, so angry at the violation of the human spirit that is going on still, right now, absolutely everywhere and all the time.

I am connecting with all the cult survivors across time and space, who just could not see what was right in front of their noses the whole time.

All of us absolutely tried our very best to make it work, but with a faulty Matrix, a destructive Matrix, the game was rigged, and we never had a chance.

We had to evolve out of it in our own sweet time, and those of us who have had this experience, we did. We finally saw it, and that, once again, is the very best we could ever have done.

Here we are.

Now we stand outside the cult.

And even here, Star Matrix comes to the rescue – especially here.

The Ultimate Heresy In The Trauma Cult

In November of 2019, I finally gathered the courage and announced Project 11 – a 12 week course to explore what happens when we deliberately access the best memories of our lives.

As an energist rather than a psychologist, I could present the case for doing such a heretical thing; of course, when we connect with happy memories, our mood in the Here & Now lifts instantly, and that is good for the living energy body in both theory and practice.

When you have two or more people thinking and talking about happy memories, the couple bubble and the group bubble effect happens, where people's energy bodies harmonise. Then we are no longer alone, feel like we are connected with each other, like each other more and general happiness ensues.

As far as I know, nobody had ever even attempted such a thing before and although it all made perfect sense in theory, we could not know what would happen in practice.

Would we all go mad?

Start hallucinating?

Somehow end up feeling worse than we had before?

I announced Project 11, gathered a group of fifty energy enabled people from all around the world and so we began.

If you are unfamiliar with Star Matrix, it starts like this.

We simply remember a moment of happiness from any time of our lives, a Star Memory, the sort of memory we would expect to be included in the "life flashing before our eyes" sequence.

We take our time to remember the memory in detail, using the Classic Game technique from SuperMind, which involves activating all six senses to get the most information out of the memory.

In order to make the conscious connection, we give this Star Memory a number, a title and a short description, inscribe it into our Book of Stars, and add the approximate age and the date.

For now, that's it. It's as simple as that. Remember some good memories and write them into your Book of Stars.

As soon as we started with this, I began to see that we were not dealing with disconnected, random memories at all, but instead with a ... Star Matrix! That's when Star Matrix got its name, and the project took its first threshold shift into something more than just taking a holiday from the endless trauma quests and trauma memories for a change.

The Star Matrix turned out to be a self concept made from a person's best moments, and when we understood this, we also understood the "Scar Matrix" which is what everyone in the trauma cult comes away with by default.

As I had long ago established the idea that we only get to know who we truly are at +10 and nowhere else, to me, this unfolding Star Matrix was much more realistic as a self concept.

The Star Matrix is also a lot more promising as an operational self concept, meaning that there is so much more to learn from this downstream of the Star Matrix itself, than the trauma based Scar Matrix could ever possibly reveal.

In the meantime, the participants of the original research project were absolutely delighted.

They found it easier and easier to remember the good moments as the project went along, and they were building new pathways in their brains.

There were also all manner of fascinating positive side effects, from "better memory" to having a new way now to communicate with other people that would naturally lead to happy energy exchanges, and this included partners, children, parents, aged relatives, strangers on a plane, co-workers and more.

Simply remembering the best moments of their lives for a change, acknowledging these Star Memories and making an official written record in their Book of Stars lit people up. It delighted them, it inspired them, it surprised them in so many ways, and it really made them happy.

I was watching all of this, taking notes and something that particularly caught my interest was that the participants were discovering a connection between their past aspects across time.

For example, a person who liked animals very much found similar Star Events from age 6, 16, 37, 56, 69 and 82.

Here was a thread that wove itself through the person's entire life and crossed all boundaries, not just of age, but of whether the person was in a relationship or not, whether they were doing well physically or not, what restrictions and challenges there were in their practical environments.

This Core Self was absolutely wonderful to experience and observe. The person was building an understanding of their true nature, one Star at a time, and beginning to appreciate themselves in a completely different way.

From my perspective, I felt the huge relief of no longer having to tell resistant people that "You are more than you think you are!" any longer.

People were discovering this for themselves, and everything they discovered was built on their own unique life experiences. This is not only the way out of the trauma cult, it is the way out of any cult at all!

In the preceding chapter I said that Star Matrix supports cult survivors from any cult profoundly, and this is how that works.

A person owns all their Stars. Of course they do, these are their own unique life's experiences. Even though people think that they had a Star Event of happiness because of another person, or because of a specific animal, or because of a specific type of landscape, or because of a special ritual in a cult, the fact is that the Star Event happens INSIDE that one person, and it only belongs to them, now, and forever.

What had previously happened (and is still happening everywhere else!) is that a person, once they are out of that damaging relationship, or that damaging job, or that damaging cult, throws the Star Events out with the bathwater and declares that entire stretch of time on their timeline as a wasteland, a terrible place where nothing good ever happened.

The fact is, however, that people do have Star Events, no matter what; and there were plenty of Star Events whilst they were in the cult.

It is important to know that people are afraid that they might go back to the cult (or the relationship, or the place, etc. etc.) if they allow themselves to remember the good times; and that is understandable.

It isn't the case, however; and I advise any cult survivor to simply remember whatever Star Events they remember, in their own unique order and sequence, just as they come, and write them down in their Book of Stars.

Eventually, it comes to pass quite naturally that a Star Event from one of these "no go zones" on their timelines pops up; and when it does, the person is ready for it and can accept it as simply one of those wonderful miracles, one of many Star Events from their real life, add it to their Book of Stars and move on.

For people who have been in cults, in prison, in the army, in relationships that started out great and then became abusive, to take back their own Stars is empowering in a way that nothing in trauma therapy could even get close to.

If you are new to this whole idea that our Star Memories not only matter, but are in fact the only memories that matter, you might be forgiven to think that we are only repressing all that trauma, and nothing good could possibly come from focusing on the best moments of our lives, giving them our full, undivided attention, so that we may learn something about ourselves and how happiness actually works in practice.

What we discovered however was that the Star Memories had the power to outshine trauma memories, to make them fade away in comparison and no longer trouble the person in question.

This was not something I had expected to happen, but it makes perfect sense from the energy perspective and worked perfectly in practice. Star Matrix raises our all important energy average.

That was the moment when Star Matrix went from a simple, happy self help methodology to also giving us the methodology for a different kind of "talking therapy" that could handle any trauma you might want to throw at it.

A Different Kind Of Talking Therapy

Modern Energy has many fascinating methods and techniques to make people feel better and to help them evolve.

I coined the phrase, "You don't have to solve it, only EVOLVE IT!" to free the practitioners of Modern Energy from the burden of somehow having to heal their client's entire incarnation in under an hour.

When a person has any kind of problem they can't fix, they get stuck, and that's like being in hell. Any evolution from that stuck state is a huge win, because now, we have proof that the situation CAN change. Now, there's hope, and we're working on how to encourage that change, so we get more beneficial change.

What Modern Energy never had before was a pure "talking therapy," meaning a form of energy healing that did not rely on tapping, teaching the client a method first such as EMO Energy In Motion, or doing direct energy healing by using healing hands.

Star Matrix is at the purely materialistic level a talking therapy.

Clients and practitioners simply talk about their Star Memories with each other, themed around whatever the client wants to evolve – be that a problem they have, or be that becoming even better at something they are already good at.

In a relationship counselling context, when there are three people involved, or in family counselling, with potentially more than three, likewise, we simply talk about the Stars and let the session unfold from there.

No tapping, no techniques, no healing – just letting people magic unfold, and brand new Star Events are the direct result.

Naturally, those among the first Star Matrix journeys, who were already professional therapists, started using Star Matrix with their clients right away.

By this time, none of us were surprised how much the clients loved this.

I am going to make a direct comparison now between what happens in Star Therapy compared to Trauma Therapy, so you may consider what might be more effective to help clients evolve and become stronger, more empowered, and more in charge of their own lives.

Client Expectation

Trauma Client: This will be harrowing and stressful, and not lead to much in the end.

Star Client: This is going to be so exciting! I can't wait to find out what we will discover!

Therapist Expectation

Trauma Therapist: I will have to hear the latest bad news from this client's life.

Star Therapist: As my Star Client tells their Star Story, it will trigger my own Star Memories! I can't wait! Together, we will learn something new and amazing!

Client State On Arrival

Trauma Client: -3 to -6 (from stressed to extremely stressed/anxious)

Star Client: +3 to +5 (from intrigued to ready for action)

Client/Therapist Connection

Trauma Client/Therapist: Rapport/Connection is not encouraged to protect the trauma therapist from having to experience the trauma client's negative emotions.

Star Client/Star Therapist: Couple bubble happens spontaneously and naturally in an atmosphere of adventure/discovery.

Treatment Flow

Trauma Treatment Flow: Stressed utterances by trauma client sets the theme for the trauma therapist to respond to until time runs out.

Star Treatment Flow: The session starts with a purpose the Star Client brings. A Star Memory is remembered. The Star Therapist assists the Star Client in fully connecting with the Star Memory. The main insight from this Star Memory is discussed, and how it is relevant for the Here & Now.

Homework

Trauma Homework: Depends on the trauma therapist and may include further trauma based activities, such as negative journaling. Medication may be prescribed.

Star Homework: The Star Client has written down the most important insight from the session, to reflect upon further in their real lives. They are also encouraged to add more entries to their Book of Stars.

I like to speak of the paradigm shift that occurs when we start thinking about our lives with six senses, rather than just five, and finally bring emotions back into the game of science and logic through the Modern Energy Chart.

I have never seen this absolute paradigm shift more clearly in action than in the context of working with clients and their Star Memories.

Star Therapy is so fundamentally different, so much easier, so much more effective and so much more fun, it's like it came from an alien planet.

It also resolves a fundamental trauma therapy problem I had observed already at the beginning of my journey – namely, that in the trauma cult there are only two states any client can inhabit, and that would be client resistance, or client compliance.

As there wasn't even a concept to describe a client who was actively engaged in the process of therapy, inspired, fully co-operative and bringing their own intelligence. intuition and creativity to the therapy party, I had to invent a new phrase – **client avidity**.

Working with Star Memories creates that positive state for our Star Clients to be in by default!

What is so extraordinary is that the possibility of this was here all along. People were actually doing this with each other, long before I came along, observed this, and made it into a pattern that can be taught and learned.

What is also important to note is that this is absolutely only the beginning.

Real Life Healing Made Possible At Last

People have lives; they have timelines.

What I have never seen addressed or tried to be addressed is to put people's entire life into some kind of context that makes sense overall, and give us human beings a way to use the information from the past to plan a trajectory into the future.

One of the objections from the trauma cult I keep hearing is that there is no use remembering "the glories of the past," because that's all gone now, and right here & now, we're sitting in the ashes of our traumas.

I find that amusing, because if there's no point in remembering the glories of the past, then what's the point in remembering all the traumas?

One of the questions I asked myself whilst I was still inside the trauma cult and took it for granted that everything that was happening there made some sense, somewhere along the line, even if I personally didn't "get it," was this.

If trauma is where it's at, then why is nobody ever making an entire timeline and mapping out all the trauma on a graph, so you can at least get an overview and a sense as to what happened when and where, in the right order and sequence?

Why is this trauma thing so utterly haphazard?

Why is every trauma treated like a disconnected island state in the person's existence?

Where are the connections between the traumas, the meta patterns?

Could it be that the very fact that people are entrained in the trauma cult, it stresses them out so much that they can no longer see the bigger picture?

Be that as it may, I did start to map trauma across the entirety of people's lives, and that was extremely difficult to do. Indeed, it never made sense at all until finally the Guiding Stars came into the picture.

Now, instead of only just mapping trauma on the timeline, we could start to map EVENTS instead.

I absolutely love this beautiful example of "increasing the complexity" - take a timeline, and add all the meaningful events, and soon enough, it ceases to be that ridiculous, reality-reduced timeline with nothing but trauma on it, and becomes far more realistic.

You can literally sense in your body, with your true sixth sense, how you start to relax as more and more events are added to the timeline.

Yes, that makes sense …

Reality divergence is being alleviated.

I believe that as thinking human beings we need to make some kind of sense to our lives, the entirety of our lived experiences, and that this is actually extremely important for us to function.

Trying to map traumas, Guiding Stars, paranormal events, healing events, miracle expansions and so forth is indeed very complex, for a person, for a client, for a therapist, but we don't actually need to do that.

The "life flashing before your eyes" that ONLY CONTAINS STAR EVENTS is the answer.

The Star Events are the best and highest experiences, so how about we use those to map our lives up to this point?

Instead of a timeline, we are dealing with a StarLine instead.

Again, for all of the infinite problems the trauma therapy has created, we have a beautiful, elegant, easy resolution.

Star Memories are completely unlike trauma memories.

They are steady, resonant, full six sensorama, sequential, and so, so information rich.

As they are also full of energy, they raise the person up the Modern Energy Chart right here, right now, and so now the person is far more intellectually capable than they were when they were stressed out of their minds.

The person can understand, learn, make connections and have really powerful AHA! moments which are brand-new Star Events in their own rights.

Creating a StarLine is easy, natural, and happens quite automatically once we have a few dozen entries in our Books of Stars.

StarLine Therapy puts people back in charge of their entire incarnation, and solves that old problem of trying to map a person's entire life to find the connections between the Star Aspects, which, all together, ARE that person.

There's more. Where trauma therapy creates a timeline that predicts more future trauma to come, the StarLine predicts there will be future Stars.

We can prove that because there always were Stars – even in the DarkFields, our term for a stretch of the timeline which we think of as having been the bad times, the bad days.

We own our Stars. We always did. They are the key to who we are, what we are about in this life, and in the end, they even give us our spiritual immortality back – not through dogma, but simply by personal, inevitable discovery.

Your own lived experience holds the secret to who you really are, your one true Core Self, which reveals itself in your Star Moments.

Your Core Self is real, it is right, it is true, and I can prove it – through your own memories.

11: The Star Of Hope

I have been publishing my findings, every step of the way, since I first realised that the invisible something was real in 1993.

It is true that I have been entirely fascinated with all the things you can DO, practically, with the methods and techniques I discovered to improve the condition of the poor neglected human energy body; and on this journey, there were such marvellous discoveries around every corner, around every bend in the road.

Just Art Solutions, all by itself, is the most superb application of creativity to finally stop endlessly reporting on the problems, and instead, move forward and out of the problem state - "Don't paint the problem (again!), paint the SOLUTION."

The endless reporting of the problems in and of themselves is how the trauma cult functions. Our societies are literally stuck in the fish tank of insanity, where we report the problems, over and over, but nobody seems to ask for the solution.

We can tune into any type of news feed, in any modality, on any platform, and all we ever get is the reporting of the problems, with no solutions being offered.

In 2012, I became extremely concerned with the sharp increase of stress in our societies, and did my best to create the solution to this – Modern Stress Management, based on our emotions, based on our living energy bodies, with simple, effective techniques that anyone can use. This is something I would recommend to any company, any organisation, any institution which has been ravaged by the extremely divisive, entirely trauma based corporate trainings that were all the rage for the last few years, to bring the people back together, refocus them on the solutions, and give them the methods they need to implement these with energy and volition.

This is what I do, this is what I have always tried to do – to create solutions to the problems we human beings are dealing with. Adding that missing component of energy, with emotions as our true 6th sense, creates that paradigm shift we needed all along, helps to connect the dots and shows us the way out of the fish tank of insanity, gives us brand new paths directly into better states of being.

Star Matrix was the final piece in my personal research program, and five years later, the Star Matrix project was concluded to my satisfaction.

Of course, we were all super delighted with Star Matrix when we first started with it, but as you know by now, I am well aware of the "early gains" when we switch from one Matrix to another, and I need to know what happens long term before I am ready to say, "Yes, this was good idea, it has proven itself with real people, living in the real world. It is beneficial and I am now ready to take it out into the world."

Focusing on the best memories of our lives has improved the mental and emotional health of the participants, has improved their self esteem, their self confidence, and, most importantly, their human relationships with their friends, families and colleagues.

Star Matrix has accomplished the research goal from 2010 – how we can ***permanently*** improve our all important energy average.

As these results became apparent over the last five years, I myself became more and more unhappy at what I was hearing and seeing outside our research program.

Mental health statistics were showing ever worsening trends.

Different groups within society were becoming more and more radicalised.

People were making a living playing out ever more extreme insanity on social media.

The will to experience better mental and emotional health seemed to become lost, and seemed to have become replaced by crazy attention seeking behaviour, and endless abreactions.

All manner of cults seemed to be forming, with ever more radical and truly disturbing ideas.

Social discourse was becoming more and more anti-social.

Clearly, the stress levels in the modern world had run completely out of control.

And all of that was happening before the two year catastrophe in slow motion which unfolded from 2020 onward, and which is still reverberating inside all of us to this day.

The Catastrophe In Slow Motion

This book is entitled, "How I Escaped The Trauma Cult," with the subtitle, "... and how you can too, if you want to."

Since 1993, when my young aspect learned how the world really works in science through research and personal experience, I have become what is called "a conspiracy theorist" - I like to think of myself as a conspiracy realist instead.

I posit that every conspiracy realist has had a similar experience, a special moment when their old world view crumbled, and was never the same again.

"Trust The Science" they told us, over and over again.

We might consider that if that experience with the dog food study had never happened to me, I might have trusted the people who told the world to trust the science too.

But that did happen, and so I did not.

I could not rationally accept that a brand new virus could pop up and a safe and effective treatment could be rolled out to the ENTIRE WORLD within such a short time.

That is simply not possible outside of a fairy tale or a fantasy movie.

It is also not possible to inject the entire population with the same thing, and not have some people in this population who will have a strong negative reaction, and it literally doesn't matter how inoffensive any substance might appear. Personally, I do just fine with peanuts, strawberries, pollen, seafood and antibiotics, but that is not so for everyone in the population.

But that's not even the end of it.

In my world, there are these invisible, ignored, neglected, starving, maltreated energy bodies, which are already stressed and which are transmitting their pain and suffering through chronic emotional stress, irrational behaviour and psychosomatic pain.

What happens to these energy bodies when you inject them with a pathogen and the immune system goes haywire?

That is a good question, and leads to other questions, such as what the effect of psychopharmaca on the living energy body might be; I hope that future researchers will take a look at that.

In the meantime, the catastrophe in slow motion was one gigantic attack on the human energy body, the human spirit.

Terrified of themselves or their loved ones dying of the plague, locked in their homes, forbidden to pray, sing or dance together; robbed of their human rights and their agency altogether; constantly bombarded with messages designed to increase fear and terror on all fronts ... It was then and is right now absolutely appalling.

And nobody seems to know or care that the human spirit itself is under attack in a way that we have never seen before.

At least in my little energy bubble, we kept our spirits up and I did my best to provide practical means and methods to help people rise up on the energy chart and keep their energy bodies stable. I ran the Energy Show on Sunday mornings live and created a free program for all comers, The Power of the Positives, to brighten our spirits, and of course, the Star Matrix research was ongoing and provided us with wonderful, brand new Star Events during those long days of isolation.

A happy energy body is the foundation for a functioning immune system …

All through that, the trauma cult kept running harder and harder, like a runaway train that we can all see eventually leaving the tracks altogether and ending in a big crash at the bottom of the mountain.

And what did the field that is supposedly responsible for the mind come up with in response to this overwhelming crisis of stress, fear, pain, anger and suffering?

More mental health diagnoses; more medication; and the adoption of critical theories in the training of the next generation of practitioners.

Thanks a lot, psychology.

After thirty years of keeping out of that completely, focusing on my own work and ignoring the nonsense happening in that field, what took place before and during the catastrophe in slow motion I found it harder and harder to ignore.

I was becoming angry. I was becoming radicalised. Finally, the time came in early 2024 that I could not be silent about it any longer.

I appreciate that this is going to be highly controversial, but I have to say it publicly now.

Psychology is a failed field.

Psychology Is A Failed Field

The word "psychology" means "the study of the soul."

Since its inception, psychology has entirely failed to make any progress whatsoever in the study of the soul.

Not only has it failed to produce any workable theories as to what a soul is, what it's good for and how we may expect its functions to manifest in human beings; it has also completely and utterly failed in producing any practical downstream methods, techniques and applications to help the citizens in moments of need or crisis.

Psychology does not have a workable definition of emotions, and neither does it have a workable, useful definition of "the mind." It has failed to unlock the incredible power of both the conscious mind as well as that of the energy mind (previously known as the "sub" or "un" conscious mind) to provide direction and create solutions.

Psychology has entirely failed to explain the cause and effect between emotion, behaviour, thought and physicality; it does not have even the beginning of a theory of mind, body and spirit.

Psychology is not a science; it is a pseudo-science that is neither producing a decent body of knowledge, nor any benefits for society at large – quite in the contrary. The countries in the world which have the most psychologists are also the countries in the world with the most mental illness in the population.

70% of all the so-called "studies" in psychology were conducted on psychology students. Now students in and of themselves are a most peculiar group of youngsters, even among the peers at their age who are not psychology students; and that in and of itself puts a massive question mark over any result that is obtained from such a group.

Much worse, however, is that not even a single one of these so-called studies factored in the stress levels of their participants.

When a person is at -4, that same person will give completely different answers and show completely different behaviours to that self same person at +7. Their ability to understand questions, solve cognitive problems, engage in social behaviours and everything else that a human being can possibly demonstrate changes according to the states of the test subjects, and if you do not understand this basic fact of life, or fail to factor it in, not a single one of these studies nor the statistics those produce can be taken seriously.

Unlike other fields of science that may well "stand on the shoulders of giants," psychology stands of the shoulders of people who neither understood emotions nor had the first clue how the energy mind actually works on the one side, and on the other, on people who tortured various animals in their research laboratories, and even their honest studies often came to entirely the wrong conclusions. Many more engaged in that process of cutting off the reports from the experiments before the negative consequences were becoming abundantly clear for all to see.

Current theories on stress management, for example, are still based on a piece of research from 1908, conducted by two scientists who electro-shocked rats in New York[xiv], as electricity was all the rage back then.

So-called Positive Psychology, which is finally acknowledging that "mental health is more than the absence of mental illness," is still psychology and entirely hamstrung by the conventions of the entire field, the absence of definitions, the lack of understanding how emotional states directly create mental expression, and most of all, by its desperate need to chase scientific respectability via P-values, which distorts their methods away from serving the clients and skews the techniques so they should show statistical results in meta analysis as their first priority.

That's just the tip of the iceberg of the problems with psychology theory and practice, and I have had enough of seeing the smug trauma grifters on the various social media platforms, telling the general public and innocent children how to spot the tens signs they too have Autism, that their parents or their partners are narcissists, how Mindfulness Meditation can get you over your childhood trauma, or to suggest journaling about everything that upsets you, twice a day.

I've had enough of the celebration of mental illness; I have had enough of social media users endlessly echoing the trauma entrainment and the algorithms feeding it back into the streams, I had enough of Complex PTSD, I've had enough of "In order to ascend, you need to descend."

We need one single change, and we need it now.

In order to ascend, you have to ascend.

In order to feel better, you need to move up on the Modern Energy Chart. It is the only way.

In order to be stronger, smarter, happier and healthier, you need to move up the Modern Energy Chart - and in order to finally heal all the trauma, we need to bring in the Stars.

In order to understand who we really are, we must, must, must stop staring at when it all goes so hideously wrong, and start looking at where things are going right, to inspire us, to empower us, to show us the way out of the fish tank of insanity.

The Good Therapists In The Bad Trauma Cult

I want to pick up on something that I have said earlier, but it's important to highlight it and expand upon it further.

The reason that any "talking therapy" ever worked at all and in the first place is that sometimes, something happens between the client and therapist, in spite of all the barriers placed between them in the practice of talking therapy, that I call "people magic."

Sometimes, two people get together. They enter into deep rapport with each other, form a couple bubble as their energy systems harmonise and combine into something that is more than the sum of their parts.

When that happens, people become able to think with more than their lonely single minds. Creative solutions may occur. Star Events of understanding, of connection, of evolution come into being.

Depleted energy systems re-activate as they are finally being nourished.

Energy body healing can occur spontaneously. A change of heart occurs and the change of mind follows, and it is a spectacular Star experience.

This can and does happen in talking therapy – but it is not to the credit of psychology when it does.

It is to the credit of an individual human being and their partner in this process.

Psychology has been falsely taking credit for people magic, and used this to shore up the fact that its own theories and practices are completely unsound in every way possible.

I would call on any good therapist who does what they do in order to actually help people to take some time and remember now when something extraordinary did happen with a client.

Remember your Star Moments with your clients.

When and where did something extraordinary happen? HOW did that happen? What did you do, what did you feel, what did you say?

Reflecting on the Star Moments with clients and taking that right back as lived experience of how things work between real human beings – not between stupid, broken, trauma riddled worm clients and oh so much better educated, all knowing "trust the science" mind doctors – is the first step towards escaping the trauma cult, rejecting the lore of psychology, and starting to understand what emotional healing really is, how it works, and how it is done.

When many more such experienced people start to talk about their Star Stories, their lived experience, with each other, meta patterns will emerge that point the way as to how talking therapy, which is nothing but real energy work in disguise, should be conducted.

The therapists themselves are the first and major victims of the trauma cult.

This starts right at the beginning, when a youngster decides they need to know more about their own problems and enrols in the study of psychology – only to be confronted with incomprehensible nonsense for theories, and having to learn all about statistics to make any of it scientific, somehow. This filters out those who had hoped for more, for better, who will give up on this insanity and leave; those who remain, are further entrained into the trauma cult, step by step, all the way.

They grow up and never find answers or solutions to their own problems; and likewise, there are no answers they can give to their clients which make any level of sense, or produce any significantly measurable benefits beyond the meaningless P-values.

At the personal level, inside the trauma cult, of course the therapists are afraid of their clients. They are afraid of what clients might bring to the session. They are afraid that the clients will "abreact," have a nervous breakdown and the ambulance needs to be called.

They are afraid that their clients will physically attack them.

They are afraid that their clients will go home and kill someone, or kill themselves and they will get the blame for it.

The clients are afraid as well, afraid of having to relive the trauma, afraid of finding repressed trauma that is so terrifying, it will drive them insane on the spot, and afraid of the therapist, who may have strange magic powers of the mind they somehow acquired in their secret towers at university, and do something unknowable but horrific to them, somehow.

Everybody is terrified of "mental illness" itself, and nobody knows whether they are mentally ill, but everyone suspects they probably might be.

To construct some kind of safety cage for the shark attack that is a trauma based talking therapy session makes perfect sense – don't connect with the client, don't care too deeply about the client, put a desk, a clipboard, and all the invisible shields you can muster between you and the client, stay detached, stay emotionally neutral and disconnected … That's held to be normal, held to be the right thing to do, but then, highly stressed people do all sorts of things that seem to make sense to other highly stressed people.

It doesn't have to be that way.

Take away the implicit focus on the everlasting trauma, and everything changes.

Both therapists and clients do not need to get exhausted by the endless negativity that never gets any better, any longer. They don't need to burn out, or give up in desperation. Bring in the Stars and there is hope once more, there is new knowledge found, there is finally a true evolution.

Clients can love their therapists again, and the therapists can love their clients, without getting involved in unhealthy transference, counter transference and counter-counter transference.

The space of people magic allowed to happen opens up.

One Star Client described this as "When I come to see you, it's like walking in the miracle zone!"

Walking In The Miracle Zone

One of the loudest drums to beat for anyone involved in anything across Mind, Body & Spirit healing modalities is that we are not supposed to ever mention "miracles of healing."

We're not supposed to mention that, and definitely not supposed to promise that.

And I agree, when a person is in the latest stage of cancer, to promise physical healing is probably not going to work out. This doesn't stop people from seeking out those who promise this regardless, but that's a story for another day.

A miracle to an individual person is a threshold shift, a personal breakthrough, something that produces this result:

Now, things are possible that were never possible before.

When we re-focus from the trauma to the Star Memories, now, things are possible that were never possible before.

Take loving yourself, for example.

Loving a miserable trauma victim aspect is very hard; and even harder to love yourself when all you are is a walking monstrosity of scars upon scars upon scars.

Loving a high energy Star Aspect could not be easier or more natural; and it gets ever easier to love yourself when you start to understand that you too have a real Star Matrix, that is unique, all your own, and absolutely real.

Please note, the saying goes, "Now, things are possible that were never possible before."

The scarred trauma victim is impossible to love; but not only is the Star Matrix self possible to love (which was never possible before!), it is easy.

Easy, natural, obvious and amazing.

It's a real WOW when that happens, when the first few Star Memories have been recovered, and they start to connect.

Self love is possible. Self admiration, understanding of the self, coming consciously into harmony with the self and with one's own life. Developing self respect which is said to precede being respected by other people.

All of that was never possible before in the trauma cult that kept all the victims going round and round in ever tightening, never ending loops inside the fish tank of insanity.

What is so extraordinary is that this was always not only possible, but easy.

You just need to choose where you want to place your attention.

Our conscious minds have such power!

A true science of what people can do with this gift from the Great Creative Order would be a wonderful, wonderful addition to the knowledge base of humanity.

Indeed, the mind does deserve its own field of study – and this becomes practically possible when we factor in the effects of the living energy body, and make it our business to find out how a normal human mind functions at above +5.

In order to have any chance to get there, first we need to say farewell to the cult of trauma, step outside of that destructive matrix, and re-focus on what really matters in life – and that would be love.

Now it is all good and well to say that "Love is all we need ..." and it has been said, many, many times before, by many, many people across the ages of humanity – but how do we get there?

And here I offer us all a great big bright white star of hope – Star Matrix is the way.

That's how we get there.

Each Star Memory is a direct personal connection to love itself.

There is a ray of love that illuminates each and every Star Memory and gives us the lived experience of love – of being in love, with another person, with another being, with an animal, with a landscape, with the sky, with the stars above, and sometimes, with life itself.

It is this experience of being in love with the Great Creative Order itself that stands tall and strong against the chaos of stress, confusion, pain, all of which are nothing but the symptoms of the absence of love.

Through our own Star Memories, we regain the truth and the power of our human existence – simple, pure, and perfect.

Star Matrix is the way.

12: I Can See Your Stars

I finally escaped the Trauma Cult for good, and forever, the moment I wrote my very first personal entry into my own Book of Stars.

I remember it well. I had a lovely spiral bound notebook which I had been keeping for a special, but as yet unknown, purpose.

I had decorated it with eight pointed stars and the words, PROJECT 11, cut from silver holographic foil, and on the first page, I had written very carefully,

This Book of Stars

belongs to

Silvia

I could sense that I was doing something wonderful, something right, something that could be tremendously exciting.

I remember how it FELT to write the first entry, No. 1.

My aspect must have been four years old at the time, and had escaped the house at sunrise in the summer in her nightgown, walking down a deeply rutted country lane, across a valley with a little stream at the bottom. Walking up the other side, it had rained in the night and little rivulets of water were running down across the sand and rocks of the lane, a miniature world which was entirely fascinating.

The little child found that by placing the rocks, the little rivers would change their course; new landscapes, new worlds could be created.

Then there was that moment when the child looked up, across the valley, and the little houses on the other side were the same size as the stones in her hands, and she understood that these houses were placed there by people, that they were movable just the same, and that it was possible to change the world.

It was a most extraordinary experience and the world was never the same again. I knew from that moment forth that not only houses that seemed so heavy and eternal could be moved, built, rebuilt; but also all the other things that were held to be so immutable, rules, ideas, concepts, in fact, everything made by human minds and hands, could be moved – by human minds, and hands.

I had thought about this memory once in a while because it would flash up across the decades, but by writing it into my Book of Stars, I knew that something significant had happened. I knew this because I could sense it in every cell of my body.

There is real magic in writing down words; and officially acknowledging and accepting your own Star Memories is life changing. I have no other words for it.

This simple act is the step across the threshold. When you do this, you are saying to yourself, and the entire multiverse, that you are now willing to find out who you really are. It acknowledges that we don't know this yet, and it also acknowledges that whatever we might have thought about ourselves and other people could be entirely wrong.

If you want to escape the Trauma Cult, once and for all, this is how it's done.

Take an inventory of your Star Moments long before you take your final breath. The plane crash survivors said that the experience of their own Star Moments changed them for the better; finally explained to them what their life had been all about.

We human beings have such extraordinary minds, and we do not have to wait until the end of our lives to get a better sense of self, and of our individual destinies.

Star Matrix is the way out of the Trauma Cult.

I offer it to you with all my heart and hope.

We Have The Power To Create Stars

Our journeys through life are absolutely extraordinary.

The way our human totality works, when it is allowed to work the best it can, is absolutely extraordinary.

We can regain a sense of how amazing we are, each one of us, and all together as well, when we come home to our Stars and reject the cult of trauma.

Reject trauma therapy, the trauma culture, the trauma art, the trauma madness, yes; but this goes much further.

Instead of creating lives so we can avoid trauma, we need to refocus our lives to create more Stars instead. Stars for ourselves, first of all and of course; but also to make it our business to create Stars for other people, be this as parents, as friends, as members of our society; as teachers, as healers, as therapists, as politicians, as bankers, as lawyers, as doctors, as mail delivery people, as shop assistants, as strangers in the street.

It is in our power to touch and move other people in such a way that they may experience a Star Event that will absolutely evolve them, make them wiser, happier, just … more than they ever were allowed to believe about themselves.

If you read this and think, "Oh, I couldn't do that, I wouldn't know how …" I would ask you to go to your own lived experience, and to a memory when a Star Event happened, because you were there.

Take a little time and really remember how that was, how that happened, and how it made you feel.

Star Matrix proves that we have a Core Self that never actually changes at all, no matter what has happened in your life, and no matter what is still to come.

From this we learn that we cannot change people, but we can change people's timelines. We can make a difference to other people's futures, to the experience of their incarnations in this life.

You don't have to be some kind of therapist to do that; every human being has the power to affect every other human being they ever meet.

This power isn't isolated to a single person; that stranger you smiled at might have been on the way to the motorway bridge to end it all, but because you did, he regained hope.

He did not jump, did not cause a major accident, nobody else was injured. The road wasn't closed, people did not miss appointments that would bring their lives upon a new road – it is literally incalculable what a single act of people magic can set into motion.

Every one of us has this extraordinary power over the timelines of unknowable people, now and in the future.

Inside the trauma cult, we are all hapless victims of our circumstances; we have no agency, we have no magic, are of no consequence. Literally nothing could be further from the truth.

Every single one of us creates consequences for each other, all the way and all the time. Picking up on this extraordinary power to do something good in the world, to assist our fellow travellers as best we can, and having that be a part of our missions becomes reality – and that is a true paradigm shift in self empowerment.

We stop being the eternal trauma victims, and become heroes instead.

And here's another and possibly the most wonderful thing that happens once you have escaped the cult of trauma and are on the other side of it, supported by your very own, absolutely unique Star Matrix.

The True Meaning Of Ascension

One of the things I adore about the world of Star Matrix is that it doesn't take long at all to change our minds.

Unlike the convoluted attempts of positive psychology to try and think our way out of stress states, which is so difficult if not entirely impossible to do when you are inside a state of stress, it seems that our natural systems spring into action and support our Star Matrix behaviours, every step of the way.

I am reminded here of a Star Story I heard when my aspect was only 21 years old, and a teacher told of the old fruit tree that is pruned to go sideways along the wall of a castle for three generations of gardeners, who cut its branches, and tie down every little shoot with ropes and wires. 75 years the fruit tree has been trained, but this year, there is no gardener, and the fruit tree immediately grows all its new shoots from its mangled branches straight back up, towards the light.

The fruit tree never "learns," and I believe our human systems are like that.

So we have been brainwashed all our lives, and the three generations before us by now, to believe in trauma, and focus only on trauma. We have been trained to believe that it is even natural for human beings to focus on the bad, instead of the good.

You may think it will take at least 20 years of heavy, incessant, daily hard work for you to laboriously grow those new connections, pathways in the brain, to start thinking in the right direction at last, but that is not the case.

Within a few weeks of starting to add Star Memories to our Books of Stars, it begins to happen that we spontaneously remember helpful positive memories in our daily lives. The idea of asking someone about something good that happened to them recently as a conversation starter and direction pops into our minds as if from nowhere.

It is as though our totality has been waiting all this time to do the right thing, and as soon as permission is given, it naturally happens that we turn towards the light, regain our true nature, just like the old fruit tree who never learned a thing from 75 years of forcing it to grow in the wrong direction.

This sort of radical change begins to happen not only within ourselves, how we think and feel about ourselves, but also in how we look at other people.

In the trauma cult, we are entrained to look at another person and to start wondering what their traumas might be.

If we were trained to be trauma therapists, or New Age healers, we know that we do that; the rest of the population has been brainwashed to do that with the full on immersion in the therapy culture with the story being told in song and tale, all the time, and all around.

I said during the first time I ran the StarLine Therapy[xv] project: "Instead of thinking of your client as a sack full of trauma, sitting on your couch, we are looking at our clients as containing many, many precious Stars –

and among them may be one that is hugely relevant to me and my own evolution!"

Before I go further with that, please take a moment and imagine any person before you, and as they stand there, saying to yourself, "I want to see your Stars."

I want to see your Stars because …

- They will show me who you truly are.
- Your Stars are amazing – I could learn so much from each and every one of them!
- Your Stars might contain the very Stars I am missing from my own Star Matrix!

Imagine, if you will, that you do that with every person you are going to meet for one week, starting from today.

Would that change the way you think about other people?

When you change the way you think about other people, does that also change the way you think about yourself?

When your thinking and feeling about other people, and you, has changed, evolved, we could say, would that also change the way you think and feel about humanity itself?

I invite you to try this for yourself.

To love a person that is nothing but a sack of trauma is very hard. It's easy enough to feel sorry for them, but that's not love. We look down on them, devalue them, have low expectations of them, have little or no hope.

We may also feel afraid of them, because trauma makes people do bad things, right? That's also the absence of love, manifest.

However ...

When we begin to conceptualise other real, living people as a collection of Stars that is still ongoing, and that those Stars will survive their physical death and go on to form the basis of their afterlife, something quite wonderful happens naturally.

It's a completely different way to interact with people, and it makes finding them interesting easy.

Interest is the first connection through which our attention flows to them.

Our attention is life giving energy for their starving, neglected energy bodies.

And yet, there are the Stars .... nobody can take those away; no trauma, no accident, no illness, no misfortune can ever eradicate them or even touch them in the slightest.

As we pay with more attention, more fascinating things become revealed, and in turn, interest turns to fascination – our attention becomes purer. If we allow this to happen, a threshold shift occurs and we are loving the Star Person who stands before us.

Don't be afraid to fall in love – we don't nearly do that often enough to learn more about love, what it is, how it works, how it can heal us and uplift us.

Through Star Matrix, I have come to the following conclusion.

"It doesn't matter if anyone ever loved you – what counts is how much you have loved, and how deeply."

I said right at the beginning that love is the most powerful force in the universe.

Perhaps I'm wrong – but for sure, love is real, and the presence or the absence of love decides whether we human beings live in heaven, or in hell.

I would posit that love is the most important topic of research and investigation there could ever be; and that for each one of us to figure out how to do love right is an incarnational challenge that would change the world if more people would take up that research, that task.

From A New Past There Arises A New Future

Remembering and re-connecting with the Star Events of your past changes the story of your life – it changes simultaneously the past, the present AND the future.

I think of this in terms of every person has their own version of their book of life.

People try to make sense of things; connect cause and effect, based on the evidence and experience they have.

Thanks to the trauma cult, their books of life are both limited, and incomplete. As the story needs to make sense, the chapters which have not yet been written, must be connected to and based on all the chapters that have come before; if they did not, nothing would make sense and we would literally go crazy.

When we start our own Books of Stars, we quite literally begin a process that changes the story of our lives that we have been telling ourselves. .

It starts with the past, to be sure; but the interaction with the Star Events has an instant effect on the Here & Now, on the present. It raises us up on the Modern Energy Chart; and now, we think, feel and do differently.

This in turn creates a different future – it simply can not not do that.

And this is what people need, and what people want: to feel better, right Here & Now; and to have a renewed sense of hope for the future.

Star Matrix gives us all of that, in the most direct, easy and delightful way possible.

It took me over 30 years to finally escape the trauma cult, but I did find the way out, and now, you can too – if you want to.

Love & Logic

So here, we come to the time when I am writing this.

I have spent my entire life trying to figure out what's going on with people.

Bringing back the human spirit, the living energy body, is alpha and omega to make progress now.

Understanding that we do not just have five senses, but six, and the sixth sense are our emotions, creates a paradigm shift and represents a true miracle expansion – now, ***things are possible that were NEVER possible before***, under the old loveless paradigm.

Making love logical was my task, and I have done the best I could with that.

Love and logic, which seem at such odds with one another, become closer and closer together as we rise up on the Modern Energy Chart, and at +10, in our Star Moments, they become one and the same.

I wanted a Matrix built on love that would empower the people who engage with it, and Star Matrix gave me that final piece, where it takes the theory right back to the lived experience of every single individual human being and becomes instead of a fairy tale, a dogma or something you have to have blind faith in, an inevitable discovery that human beings will naturally make, time and time anew.

In order to solve all the myriad of problems and challenges that humanity faces, I decided to create a system that puts individual people in the best position to be able to exist as themselves, and to connect with other people to form these amazing group bubbles, where people get to think with more than their own one single lonely brain.

Rather than adding yet another system of philosophy that cannot begin to work for us unless we sort out why people do what they do first of all, I want to leave this to people who are less stressed and more empowered so they can find their new, creative, intelligent and most of all, love based solutions.

The Modern Energy Chart is our guide; both to evaluate the lore of the past, as well as where we humans need to be in order to unlock our true creativity, our true intelligence and our infinite capacity to love. The Modern Energy Chart maps not only individuals or groups such as families and businesses, but also entire civilisations, and here too, it shows us the right direction to move towards better states of being.

The Modern Energy Chart shows us the +10 moments, but they are not an illusion or a figment of false hope. Not only are the +10 moments available to every human being alive, we have all had so many of those already!

The realisation that I can prove this through everyone's own lived experience was the key moment which crowned my life's work – I literally had a flash up where I saw the bright white eight pointed star placed right at the top of my tree of life, and I heard, "Star Matrix is the way!".

Start Today – Star Matrix Is The Way!

If you too are now ready to leave the cult of trauma behind, and start to focus on what were always the most important nexus moments in our lives, I welcome you and ask you now to start your own Book of Stars.

Focus on your own Star Events now. You can't go wrong with that. It is easy and natural.

If you have children, draw their attention to their own best moments, for example, by asking them about the best moment of the day before they go to sleep at night. I would love for families to create shared Books of Stars where entries are agreed by everyone.

If you have a partner, take a moment, once in a while, and say to yourself, "I want to know your Stars!" Partners have a plethora of shared Star Events in their relationship they can refer to in order to re-connect after arguments, re-build their couple bubble, and they also have all manner of Star Events that the other has never heard of, but would be delighted to discover. Where, when and how their Star Events came into being is also, of course, a great help in planning future activities that might result in more shared Stars – and that's exciting, even just to think or talk about.

If you have ageing relatives, encourage those to start their Book of Stars too. You will be amazed just how much joy it gives them, how it brightens their spirits and they may even share some of the treasures and riches of their Star Moments with you.

If you are a teacher, ask your students for the best moment in the class. It is a great way to end the class and learn what works, and that is cumulative over time with every class you give.

If you are a carer, ask the people in your care about their Stars and watch them come to life before your eyes and know you have done something truly remarkable – you have activated real people magic.

If you have always wanted to help people feel better, then consider becoming a Star Therapist. Beyond the ability to delight and empower your Star Clients and any financial rewards, you will be receiving precious Star Stories, and be inspired and delighted by what you learn through them about yourself. Begin your journey by engaging with the exercises in my book, Star Matrix, and taking an online test to gain your Star Matrix Foundation certificate.

Star Matrix is the 180' "rEvolution" that was always needed for not just emotional healing, but in fact, emotional evolution – the real growing up of our living energy bodies, of our spirits, something we human children have been struggling with and craving deeply since we first looked up at the stars and wondered what they are.

In our unique ability as human beings to share our Stars with one another, we have the potential for each one of us to become more than the sum of our parts.

We can learn and evolve through other people's Stars.

The natural journey from self help, to helping one other person as a healer or therapist at a time, to working with groups of people as a teacher, as a trainer, now makes perfect sense as we understand it is our business in this life to collect as many Stars as we possibly can!

It is my personal belief that every Star moment evolves us and adds to the strength of our living energy bodies. I further believe that we have an energy system which is not tied to the physical body, and which therefore can survive the transition into a non-physical afterlife if it is strong and healthy enough.

I believe, based on the evidence of my own lived experience, that the soul is real, and that it is fed and nourished by the Star Events of our lives, those moments when we evolve, when we learn something new and important about the true nature of the multiverse.

What is absolutely astonishing to me is that we can evolve through the Stars of other people, Stars we never experienced ourselves but when we hear the other person's Star Story, it ignites something inside us and gives us an important puzzle piece for our own evolution.

Every single Star Story, experienced by any human being anywhere on this planet, at any time, is a true treasure that has the power to enlighten us all.

This breaks the barriers of age, race, gender, religion, education and brings us back together in our shared humanity, and finally gives us that space of love where we can come together as the one single human race.

When we start creating stories, art, law, systems of thought and interaction based on our Stars rather than our pain, suffering and trauma, we all evolve together at last.

Your Star Memories are the true Treasures & Riches of your life, as are mine; they are precious, they are powerful and they are important, and when we put them together, something astonishing cannot help but emerge.

Discover yourself, start with your own true Core Self and find out who you really are.

When you are looking at other people, start to want to know their Stars, because only those will tell you who that person really is, just the same.

Start thinking about your ancestors, and theirs, not in terms of their traumas but of their Stars instead to gain a different perspective on humanity itself.

Look to the Stars for the power, the information, the hope and the love we all have been seeking our whole lives long.

That is the way to truly escape the nightmare labyrinth, the fishtank of insanity, the cult of trauma, and to enter a space of such possibility and potential, it takes my breath away.

Silvia Hartmann

March 21st, 2024

"Star Matrix is the way."

Silvia Hartmann's STAR MATRIX

Best Seller

www.StarMatrix.org

i   The Harmony Program, Silvia Hartmann 1993
ii Project Sanctuary, Silvia Hartmann 1996
iii Adventures In EFT, Silvia Hartmann, 1998 1st Ed – 2003 - 8th Ed
iv The Guiding Stars Paper, 2000; later integrated into The Advanced Patterns of EFT, 2004
v   Events Psychology, Silvia Hartmann, 2008
vi Energy EFT (Book), Silvia Hartmann 2011; Energy EFT Foundation Course, Energy EFT Master Practitioner Course 2011
vii History of the DSM https://www.ncbi.nlm.nih.gov/pmc/articles/PMC3282636/
viii https://www.theguardian.com/lifeandstyle/2016/may/15/my-therapist-suicide-julia-pierpoint-psychology-grief-coping Julia Pierpont
ix How Big Pharma Makes Healthy People Sick | ENDEVR Documentary 16:51
x   The Evil Scissors from rEvolution, Silvia Hartmann 2016
xi Oceans Of Energy, Silvia Hartmann 2003; EMO Energy In Motion, Silvia Hartmann 2016
xii The Third Field, Keynote Speech by Silvia Hartmann, 2011 https://goe.ac/the_third_field.htm
xiii The Power Of The Positives (Book & Video Course) Silvia Hartmann 2020
xiv Yerkes Dobson Rats – See The Trillion Dollar Stress Solution for further information.
xv StarLine Therapy by Silvia Hartmann, 2023

Printed in Great Britain
by Amazon